Downsizing

Downsizing

Letting Go of Evangelicalism's
Nonessentials

Michelle Van Loon

William B. Eerdmans Publishing Company
Grand Rapids, Michigan

Wm. B. Eerdmans Publishing Co.
2006 44th Street SE, Grand Rapids, MI 49508
www.eerdmans.com

© 2025 Michelle Van Loon
All rights reserved
Published 2025

Book design by Lydia Hall

Printed in the United States of America

31 30 29 28 27 26 25   1 2 3 4 5 6 7

ISBN 978-0-8028-8462-6

Library of Congress Cataloging-in-Publication Data

A catalog record for this book is available from the Library
of Congress.

A bruised reed he will not break, and a smoldering wick he will not snuff out, till he has brought justice through to victory.
(Isaiah 42:3; Matthew 12:20)

For all the bruised reeds and smoldering wicks

Contents

	Introduction	1
1.	It's Time to Go	11
2.	Who's Going with You?	25
3.	Assess Your Mess	38
4.	Commit to Purposeful Pruning	52
5.	Grief Is a Part of the Process	66
6.	Chaos versus Clarity	81
7.	Sort It Out	94
8.	There Are No Shortcuts	110
9.	Saying Good-bye to Useless Things	126
10.	Freedom in Leaving Most Everything Behind	142
	Conclusion: Bride	155

Contents

Appendix: Spiritual Trauma Resources	161
Acknowledgments	165
Bibliography	169

Introduction

I'd been imagining it for three long years. I expected to feel joy when I had my first taste of freedom.

When I first told my Jewish parents shortly after I turned fifteen that I believed that Jesus is the Messiah, they told me that while I was living under their roof, they would not permit me to attend church. Though they weren't religiously observant, they were children of those forced to flee the eastern European pogroms of the late nineteenth and early twentieth centuries. As my parents came of age during and after World War II, they experienced both the American dream and the nightmare of antisemitism at the hands of "Christian" gentiles.

They viewed my decision to follow Jesus as an incredible betrayal. They hoped to starve out my seedling faith, diagnosing it as a religious fad born of teenage rebellion.

Instead, their opposition drove my tender roots deep. I resorted to guerilla tactics to feed my faith: attending a Bible study that met before school or going with friends to a Saturday night worship gathering that met at a local community center. I pirated Christian books and music into the house, listened to sermons on

Introduction

the local Christian radio station behind the closed doors of my bedroom, and, when the house was empty, watched Pat Robertson's *700 Club* on TV. When Pat asked his viewers to place their hands on the TV screen to join him in prayer for a miracle, I did. The miracle I requested again and again was to be free to go to church. I sensed God's nearness during those lonely years, but I ached for community. I loved my family of origin, but I also wanted to become a part of a new family that shared my faith.

A guidance counselor at my high school told me that if I just took a few extra classes, I could graduate a semester early. Most of the kids who opted for early graduation did so to work full time to save some money for college tuition. But leaving high school midyear was my "Get Out of Jail Free" card. I could graduate and enroll in a four-year college a couple of hours away from home as a socially acceptable way of escape.

My parents may not have been privy to my motivation, but they blessed my plan. It wasn't easy for any of us living under one roof. We all learned to be very careful to not get too close to any kind of faith-related topic, which meant we didn't talk about much of anything at all. It was like living in the no-man's-land of the 38th parallel dividing North Korea and South Korea. That strip of land, just two and a half miles wide, has served to enforce a tense political truce that has separated the families of the Korean peninsula for more than seven decades. My faith was my family's no-man's-land.

Illinois State University was 140 miles from my parents' home. The comfortable distance was one reason for choosing the school, but my primary reason was because some Christian friends from my high school were enrolled there. My initial major might have been history, but I went to college to be a part of a church in present-day 1977.

My parents took me to campus on a bleak, icy January Friday before classes started the following Monday. I hadn't yet met my roommate. Like most of the other returning students, she wouldn't be on campus until Sunday night. I was alone in the nearly empty dorm.

Introduction

As I said good-bye to my parents, I expected to feel jubilant. Instead, as I watched them drive away, a wave of grief that had been building just beneath the surface for the last three years crashed over me. My parents were gone, our relationship seemingly frayed beyond mending.

I'd counted the cost of following Jesus three years earlier. I thought I understood what the tab would be. But it took that moment in the dorm to realize that my dreams of this moment had never included the shock of cutting loose from a family that had branded me a traitor.

I prayed that the church would be waiting to welcome me with open arms.

My Evangelical Family Tree

In the five decades I've been a follower of Jesus, I have discovered that my relationship with the church is no less complicated than my relationship with my family of origin.

During those years, I've had a front-row pew from which to view many of the events, trends, personalities, fads, and theological battles that have shaped the growth of the wild, often-unruly branch of the Christian family tree known as evangelicalism. Through a number of relocations, an unquenchable spiritual hunger, various ministry roles, and my vocation as a writer, I've been a part of a wide and wild variety of evangelical subcommunities and settings during the last fifty years.

I've participated in the waning days of the Jesus Movement, immersed myself in fundamentalist faith, worshiped in Messianic Jewish gatherings, experienced the revivalism of second- and third-wave charismatic congregations, gathered in a living room for home church, experienced the rise of one of America's most influential nondenominational megachurches, became a part of the rising Anglican movement, and had pit stops along the way at other churches of all kinds, from a cult-like sect to a neo-Reformed

Introduction

outpost to a throwback mainline church that owned not one but two harpsichords in addition to its giant pipe organ.

I've been in the room where decisions were made and power was wielded in a few congregations, a seminary, and in various parachurch ministries. I'm a survivor of spiritual abuse, which is a pattern of soul-shattering manipulation, control, and punishment by a spiritual authority. I've choked on factory-produced plastic spiritual fruit of the Spirit and tasted the heavenly sweetness of the real thing—often in the very same congregation. Today, a growing number of evangelicals are heading out the doors of their churches, or at least eyeing them longingly. Some are deconstructing their faith. Others are sensing that we've arrived at a crossroads and there's no clear path forward—not without a serious recalibration.

The late Phyllis Tickle observed that about every five hundred years or so the church has a rummage sale to purge the accumulation of theological garbage and clarify the church's identity and mission for new generations.[1] The first major rummage sale took place in AD 481 when the Council of Chalcedon drew some hard lines about what it meant to believe in Christ as a response to the rise in the church of so many freelance sects and unorthodox innovations in doctrine. In 1054, the Great Schism between the Catholic and Orthodox churches became final after a couple of centuries of increasing doctrinal friction between Eastern and Western European church leaders. Then in the 1500s the Protestant Reformation swept across European churches.

Evangelicalism's roots are planted deep within the soil of the Reformation and first budded as a new expression of Protestantism during the seventeenth century. The evangelical movement gained influence in America in the decades after the Civil War. After World War II, new waves of growth in evangelical churches

---

1. Phyllis Tickle, *Emergence Christianity: What It Is, Where It's Going, and Why It Matters* (Grand Rapids: Baker Books, 2012).

Introduction

and organizations paralleled the demographic explosion known as the baby boomer generation (people born 1946–1964). In 1969, the youth-fueled Jesus Movement caught fire first in California, eventually spreading across the country. It was a turning point, and launched a dizzying array of evangelical expressions, theological innovations, and church practices over the next fifty years.

If Tickle's hypothesis is correct, the church is right on schedule for another rummage sale. The signs are all around us, particularly in the evangelical world: reports of declining attendance, stats revealing that more churches are closing their doors than launching, and the steady drumbeat of reports of morally compromised leaders. Authors Jim Davis, Michael Graham, and Ryan Burge summed up the downsizing that is occurring in most sectors of the church today: "We are currently experiencing the largest and fastest religious shift in U.S. history. It is greater than the First and Second Great Awakening and every revival in our country combined but in the opposite direction."[2]

There are lots of sound reasons for this shift, including regular reports of moral failures and abuses of power by clergy; frustration with the church's traditional positions on social issues including gender, abortion, and gay rights; the merging of faith with American Republican politics and advocacy for authoritarian government; cultural changes brought about by the rise of the digital world; and redefined notions of family . . . just for starters. But Phyllis Tickle's observation adds historical context. There's a rummage sale going on.

2. From Jim Davis, Michael Graham, and Ryan Burge, *The Great Dechurching: Who's Leaving, Why Are They Going, and What Will It Take to Bring Them Back?* (Grand Rapids: Zondervan, 2023). This quote was shared widely around the time of the book's release, so it may have come from a publicist, as it doesn't appear to be in the book in this concise form. (For a similar quotation from the aforementioned book, see Jessica Gross, "The Largest and Fastest Religious Shift in America Is Well Underway," *New York Times*, June 21, 2023, https://tinyurl.com/277hsa88.)

Introduction

I've been a part of the evangelical world since I took my first breaths of reborn life in 1974, inhaling the technicolored air of the Jesus Movement as it blew across the Midwest. Prior to that moment, I had engaged in promiscuous behavior, was drinking alone, was smoking weed almost every day, and had assembled a bag of pills I'd started carrying with me for the day I found the courage to end my unhappy life.

A friend came to school one day and announced that she'd become a Christian the night before. That conversation led to many more about God over the next few months. In those Jesus-soaked days, all kinds of people seemed to be talking about having a relationship with him. I purchased a groovy-looking Bible paraphrase called *The Way*[3] and snuck it into the house. I knew without anyone telling me that my parents would not like the part in the groovy Bible that was about Jesus. I determined to use it to read "our" Bible—what Christians called the Old Testament—while I tried for months to figure out why Jesus was such a big deal to so many people I knew at school.

When I finally decided to read the New Testament, a friend suggested I read the Gospel of John. When for the first time I read John 14:6 ("I am the Way—yes, and the Truth and the Life. No one can get to the Father except by means of me"),[4] my questions about Jesus melted wordlessly into faith in him. I knew in the marrow of my bones there was no turning back. I was following Jesus the Jewish Messiah now.

Once I was born again, I moved directly into a strange sort of faith incubator. At the time, it felt like punishment to be forbidden to do the kinds of things the other Jesus-following kids at school could do. I felt like a tourist at my occasional sneaked visits to church or Christian youth activities. My main experience of disci-

3. A youth-focused packaging of The Living Bible, first published by Tyndale in 1971.

4. The Living Bible.

Introduction

pleship was simply poring over the pages of my Bible alone in my room, learning how to mine its treasure, and discovering how to hear and obey its Author.

I supplemented that with a diet of radio preachers and TV evangelists. Most of them emphasized the importance of every individual having a personal relationship with God through Jesus. But I discovered in my Bible reading that community was essential to faith, too. God was near, and oh so gracious during my first three years alone in the incubator. But I understood instinctively that none of us are meant to live in an incubator long term. I belonged to the church, even when I was required to live in isolation from her.

Scripture and culture offer many different images of what the church is meant to be. In the decades since I left that faith incubator, I've witnessed the church in many different forms, with many different emphases. Each one attempted to highlight some aspect of what it meant to be a part of the body of Christ. Each one gained a following in evangelicalism, tapping into the holy longing within God's children for his kingdom to come and his will to be done on earth as it is in heaven.

At the same time, there have been theological fads and gimmicks in evangelicalism. There has been bad teaching. There has been abuse of power. There has been moral failure. There have been lopsided excesses and toxic emphases. We have wounded one another. We've chased others away. And in spite of ourselves and because of God's grace, we've midwifed many others to new life.

We are now in a time of reckoning. We are actively sorting through the last couple of generations of evangelicalism in the West. Only those who come after us will be able to assess whether this is a full-scale rummage sale or just a spring cleaning of a slice of the larger global church. In any case, here in America, downsizing is in progress.

To do the work of downsizing well, we must first remember. The most common word in the Old Testament for this kind of remembering is *zakar*. This word doesn't mean retrieving data

7

Introduction

from a file folder in our brain that will tell us the location of our lost car keys. It is instead a holy call to experience the story again. Remembering isn't mixing up a brew of syrupy nostalgia, nor does it erase the challenging, painful pieces of the past. It is instead an invitation to reflect on our past with the wisdom we've gained because we've lived it. Once I left the incubator nearly fifty years ago, I've been a witness. I remember.

And if you've been involved in some way with the evangelical movement at any time during your lifetime, you've been a witness, too.

Downsizing discusses a number of tributaries that have shaped evangelicalism during the last half century. Some may be as familiar to you as your old WWJD ("What Would Jesus Do?") rubber wristband. Others may seem obscure at first, at least until you take a closer look and discover how these tributaries have spilled into the movement—and in some cases, the broader culture—far beyond their sometimes-humble beginnings. I share parts of my own journey in order to frame the discussion, but my focus is to offer you some user-friendly historical and theological context for this current moment.

Using the lens of the physical downsizing process, this book will give you an opportunity to reflect on your own experience with evangelicalism, consider the legacy of this movement, lament what needs to be lamented, and think deeply about what it means to belong to the church past, present, and future. Each chapter will end with some reflection questions that will allow you—perhaps in conversation with others—to assess what, if anything, is truly worth treasuring from all that has accumulated in evangelicalism from the various trends, teachings, and groups over the last half century. I am not a prophet, nor do I have access to the cheat codes for the future that will unlock easy answers. But if enough of us begin prayerfully asking good questions, I am confident that, together, we can discover the next step (and the one after that) as we seek to follow Jesus into the future.

Introduction

Jesus once told Peter that the gates of Hades would not prevail against the community of called-out ones (Matt. 16:18). The periodic rummage sales of the past two thousand years continue to clarify what the church is as well as what it was never meant to be. Remembering well can guide us as we assess what to haul to the trash, consider what might need to be repurposed, and assess what we already possess that is worth treasuring. Downsizing makes space for what's next.

1

It's Time to Go

I once served as a writing tutor for small groups of middle-school students. To illustrate the way a single noun could paint wildly different pictures in the minds of readers, I asked the young writers to describe what they first thought when I said the word "dog." I got paragraphs describing Chihuahuas, Rottweilers, golden retrievers, and a kennel full of assorted mutts. Each one described the genus and species *Canis lupus familiaris*, but I never got the same answer twice.

The word "evangelical" is a lot like that. Before we journey through some of the specific streams and trends that have shaped evangelicalism in America over the last fifty years and influenced its expression in other parts of the world, it is of value to attempt to define what evangelicalism is. We may well end up with a gallery full of different images, but the discussion will help orient us to the variety within this spiritual genus and species.

What Does It Mean to Be Evangelical?

The word comes from the Greek word *euangelion*, which is used in Scripture to express the idea of glad tidings of salvation, good

Chapter 1

news, or the gospel. By this definition, evangelicals are people who proclaim the gospel in word and deed.

Depending on whom you query, and the context in which you do so, the word might paint a picture of people who are known for proclaiming the gospel by

- handing out gospel tracts on city streets
- feeding the homeless living in city parks
- arguing about theology on social media
- discussing doctrine in Sunday school classes
- speaking in tongues
- not speaking in tongues
- voting Republican
- avoiding politics entirely
- not drinking alcohol
- having church gatherings in bars
- dressing conservatively
- wearing T-shirts printed with Christian slogans or Bible verses
- asking Jesus into their heart
- being at church every time the doors are open
- finding fellowship, learning, and service opportunities in their communities
- boycotting Disney
- watching "safe for the whole family" Disney movies
- watching preacher Joyce Meyer on TV
- listening to John Piper sermons via podcast
- being a bunch of old hippies
- being Gen Z hipsters
- enshrining the traditional nuclear family
- having a similar divorce rate to the religiously unaffiliated
- preaching against the LGBTQIA+ community
- being fierce advocates for the marginalized in society
- living their best life now
- being so heavenly minded they're no earthly good

It's Time to Go

- acting as a cheerleader for Team Jesus
- embracing the cross

Is "evangelical" a religious category? Or might it also be a cultural category? A social category? A political category?

Those who think in terms of cultural, social, or political evangelicalism will draw a different "insider" circle in America than they would in mainland China, Brazil, or among a tiny group gathered to worship in secret in Iran. On the other hand, if we view the question through a religious lens, we will end up with a metaphorical kennel full of different kinds of canines from mutts to purebreds, but each will probably belong to the dog family.

It would be lovely if these categories were tidy slots into which we could sort out our answers. But that isn't the untamed, ever-evolving nature of evangelicalism. All those categories contribute to our understanding of what an evangelical is. And those categories to varying degrees shape the conversation about the future of evangelicalism as we reflect on what's worth keeping and what needs to be left behind.

No matter what your experience has been with evangelicalism, it is a conversation to which you're invited. Downsizing is a communal task.

Passionate Piety

When I came to faith as a teen, the irresistible draw for me was the person of Christ, expressed through the Jesus Movement. While my gateway into evangelicalism was religious, the path to that gateway was paved by cultural factors.

Since the late 1980s, the religious category has been defined by British historian David Bebbington's quadrilateral that describes evangelicalism's distinctives. The National Association of Evangelicals offers this summary of Bebbington's quadrilateral:

Chapter 1

- Conversionism: the belief that lives need to be transformed through a "born-again" experience and a lifelong process of following Jesus
- Activism: the expression and demonstration of the gospel in missionary and social reform efforts
- Biblicism: a high regard for and obedience to the Bible as the ultimate authority
- Crucicentrism: a stress on the sacrifice of Jesus Christ on the cross as making possible the redemption of humanity.[1]

Over the years, many practitioners have noted that Bebbington's idealized distinctives don't always match evangelical practice. Australian theologian Dr. Brian Harris said, "While Bebbington's priorities remain relevant, contemporary evangelicalism might be better characterised as being a community of passionate piety. While at a popular level, the doctrinal focus of the past has receded, the experience of a transforming encounter with Christ remains."[2]

That kind of transformational encounter, often coming at the point of a spiritual or moral crisis, is the primary way in which I've understood evangelicalism. A potent image that imprinted me early and continues to inform my thinking comes from a first-century conversation that took place under the cover of darkness. Nicodemus, a Pharisee who carried an extra measure of religious authority as a member of the Jewish ruling council, came under the cover of night's darkness to see Jesus. It seemed Nicodemus was concerned about marring his sterling public reputation by associating with this outsider rabbi. It also seemed obvious that he was on a personal mission to decode the puzzle Jesus presented to

---

1. "What Is an Evangelical?" National Association of Evangelicals, accessed September 27, 2024, https://tinyurl.com/yk97rz2t.

2. Brian Harris, "Beyond Bebbington: The Quest for Evangelical Identity in a Postmodern Era," Theology on the Web, accessed September 27, 2024, https://tinyurl.com/3rutrxah.

It's Time to Go

Nicodemus's peers and coreligionists. The conversation recorded in John 3:1-21 is a snapshot of a man who was simultaneously unsettled by and curious about Jesus.

When Nicodemus told Jesus that no one could do the miracles Jesus was doing unless God sent him, Jesus told Nicodemus that only those who'd been born again could see where those miracles were pointing—directly at God's kingdom.

Just as a baby emerges from a watery womb and inhales the breath of life at birth, Jesus was telling a deeply religious adult that a second birth was both possible and necessary: through Jesus, the Father was calling each person to a new life lived under the reign of God, initiated through the baptismal waters of repentance and animated by the breath of the Holy Spirit. Jesus was amplifying and illuminating the promises God had already made to Nicodemus's people—promises that Jesus would extend to all of humanity later in the same nighttime conversation when he said that God demonstrated his love for the whole world by giving his one and only Son to that world so that anyone who believed in him would have life forever with him. New birth begets eternal life (John 3:16).

Like Nicodemus, I had been born again. During the 1970s, I stepped into a world where that kind of religious language was in the ether of both politics and popular culture because the president, Southern Baptist Jimmy Carter, taught Sunday school and made no secret of his "born again" faith.[3] When he was interviewed by *Playboy* magazine during the 1976 election, Carter used religious language that would be familiar to many Christians when he confessed to harboring lust in his heart. Much of the rest of America found the Democratic governor's homespun

---

3. Carter left the Southern Baptist Convention in 2000 over the denomination's views on women but maintained his faith. A couple of pieces that explore why: "Jimmy Carter Leaves Southern Baptists," ABC News, October 20, 2000, https://tinyurl.com/332pbwu9; Philip Yancey, "The Rise and Fall and Rise of Jimmy Carter," Philip Yancey, March 2023, https://tinyurl.com/ycyp7v4k.

Chapter 1

earnestness and commitment to live his religious convictions a head-scratcher, though he went on to become president that year, benefiting less from his deep faith commitment than from the country's weariness from the choices made by its two previous Republican presidents.

If a person said they'd been born again during those days, it signaled that they may have had a personal spiritual crisis leading to a decision to commit their life to Jesus. This crisis could look like walking forward in response to an altar call at a Billy Graham crusade, praying the prayer at the end of the Campus Crusade for Christ (now rebranded as Cru) tract *The Four Spiritual Laws*, or asking Jesus to "come into your heart and forgive your sins."[4] I understood evangelicalism as a way of saying that we had a faith that was all about a personal relationship with Jesus—in other words, individual spiritual regeneration.

If I was clear in those days about what it meant to be an evangelical, I was a little fuzzy about the purpose of the church. Christian leaders tended to represent the church merely as the container that held all those born-again decisions. While I never heard this preached overtly, it was implied in all the ways in which individual commitment and preference have always been prioritized in evangelical congregations.

The notion of the centrality of the individual wasn't unique to modern-era evangelical believers. Baptist historian Thomas Kidd noted, "Christianity contained the seeds of individualism from the beginning. Even the lowliest people in society could become children of God through Christ, giving all Christians a basic claim on human dignity."[5] However, it came to the fore during the Enlightenment,

---

4. Campus Crusade for Christ was founded in 1951 and changed its name in 2011 in order to distance itself from the negative historical connotations of the word "crusade."

5. Thomas Kidd, *Who Is an Evangelical? The History of a Movement in Crisis* (New Haven: Yale University Press, 2019), 15.

It's Time to Go

which first gained traction in the 1700s. Not so coincidentally, the seeds of evangelicalism first took root at around the same time.

Within the Category, a Spectrum

Outside observers might view evangelicalism as a monolithic movement, but I've found it helpful to view the category as a spectrum of beliefs and practices. On the far end of the spectrum, you might find fundamentalist churches preaching extreme lifestyle separation from the world, embracing patriarchy, and insisting that the only trustworthy version of the Bible is the 1611 King James Version. On the other end, you might find an egalitarian-run congregation made up of tattoo artists and baristas creating new liturgies as a form of communal prayer and partnering with non-Christian community activists to work on social justice issues. In between, you might find neo-Reformed groups, nondenominational megachurches, members of Assemblies of God, and hundreds of other variations.

The far end of the spectrum came into focus at the turn of the last century in response to a theologically liberal wave of thought that washed across a number of influential Presbyterian congregations and colleges. This wave challenged academics and church members alike to reevaluate the church's relationship with the modern world, the way Scripture was read and interpreted, and advances in science and technology, particularly the rise in acceptance of Darwin's evolutionary theory. For every action there is usually an equal and opposite reaction. In the early decades of the twentieth century, the reaction to modernity was a series of lines drawn in the mud by those who hewed conservative, insisting that the Bible was without error, Scripture needed to be taken literally, and the acceptance of modern science's conclusions about life's origins and the existence of God had to be challenged.

These ideas merged with cultural concerns in those circles about the rise in technology and the loosening of moral codes,

Chapter 1

along with the already-popular Holiness teaching about the need for Christians to be different from the world around them.[6] The net result of these influences contributed to a legalistic fundamentalist subculture in evangelical Protestantism.[7]

In the aftermath of World War II, there was fresh energy for some in the fundamentalist bunker to rethink their engagement with society and other believers without diluting their theological convictions. Evangelist Billy Graham, and theologians including Harold Ockenga, John Stott, and Carl Henry, were among those who sought to reform evangelicalism and reposition it away from fundamentalism's spiritual and cultural isolationism. Many of their former fundamentalist compatriots viewed this shift toward what came to be called "generous orthodoxy" as spiritually compromised at best and departing from the faith altogether at worst.

6. This influence emerged from the Keswick movement, which was rooted in Wesleyanism. It pressed heavily for "entire sanctification" in the lives of believers and could be found in the teachings of Dwight Moody and A. B. Simpson, and in the writings of authors like Oswald Chambers and Hannah Whitall Smith.

7. Theologian Roger Olson delineated the distinctives of fundamentalist subculture: "The distinctive hallmarks of post-1925 fundamentalism are 1) adding to those essentials of Christianity non-essentials such as premillennial eschatology, 2) 'biblical separation' as the duty of every Christian to refuse fellowship with people who call themselves Christians but are considered doctrinally or morally impure, 3) a chronically negative and critical attitude toward culture including non-fundamentalist higher education, 4) emphatic anti-evolution, anti-communist, anti-Catholic and anti-ecumenical attitudes and actions (including elevation of young earth creationism and American exceptionalism as markers of authentic Christianity), 5) emphasis on verbal inspiration and technical inerrancy of the Bible as necessary for real Christianity (including exclusion of all biblical criticism and, often, exclusive use of the KJV), and 6) a general tendency to require adherence to traditional lifestyle norms (hair, clothes, entertainment, sex roles, etc.)." Roger E. Olson, "What Distinguishes 'Evangelical' from 'Fundamentalist'?" *Patheos*, December 2, 2017, https://tinyurl.com/5xmxe9zu.

It's Time to Go

Theologian Roger Olson noted, "Formally speaking, fundamentalists are evangelicals and, to liberals, anyway, all evangelicals are fundamentalists."[8] In other words, the core religious beliefs may look the same across the spectrum of evangelicalism, but those on the fundamentalist end of the scale tend to have different social lifestyle rules. When I first came to faith in Christ, the old-fashioned saying still in use in fundamentalist circles was "Don't smoke, don't chew, and don't go out with girls who do." Those lifestyle regulations functioned at the level of nonnegotiable religious dogma, and included insistence on modest clothing for women and bans on drinking, dancing, and "mixed bathing" (men and women swimming or hanging out at the beach together); playing cards, which might be used for gambling (Uno cards were OK); secular higher education; and any kind of rock music because of its "devil beat" and scandalous lyrical content.

Evangelicals who worship on the other end of the spectrum from their fundamentalist siblings may not encounter this thorny thicket of often-unwritten lifestyle rules, but most have probably scraped up against them in some form or another. It would make our categories a lot clearer if belief à la Bebbington was the only evangelical boundary marker. While belief is central, there is no way to adequately discuss the evangelicalism that is in the process of being downsized without also reflecting on how it has functioned in recent decades as a social, cultural, and political movement.

Me and My Evangelicalism?

The evangelical emphasis on the individual can make it prone to being shaped by social and cultural preferences, rather than having its primary identity derived from the church. Writer Jake Meador said, "'Evangelicalism' is chiefly a sociological movement built around

8. Olson, "What Distinguishes 'Evangelical' from 'Fundamentalist'?"

Chapter 1

consumption patterns, political identity, and attending conferences, all of which has no essential or necessary relationship to a local church, denomination, church courts, or ecclesial authority."[9]

The last major rummage sale in the church five hundred years ago birthed Protestantism—a decentralized grouping of movements without a single pope-like figure to shepherd the whole church. Instead, there were four early branches with distinctly different theologies, structures, values, and leaders: Lutherans, Calvinists, Anglicans, and Anabaptists. Written in the DNA of each of those branches was the battle cry first shouted in the high church Latin of the first Reformers: "Ecclesia reformata, semper reformanda" (The church reformed, always reforming). As those first Protestant branches began to institutionalize, a wild tangle of uncultivated evangelical sprouts budded from those boughs. Those sprouts were often rooted in disagreement with those in power over theology, practice, or the color of carpeting in the church sanctuary. As a result, there are many different evangelicalisms rather than a single, monolithic movement.

Historian Diana Butler Bass observed, "Like it or not—believe it or not—white evangelicalism is a uniquely American folk religion that has shaped our entire history, culture, and political life over the last three centuries."[10] She's not wrong, as White evangelicals grab political and cultural headlines in popular media, but evangelicals as a group aren't quite so easily categorized. A 2016 Public Religion Research Institute study of more than 100,000 Americans reveals a far more diverse picture of the racial makeup of self-identified American evangelicals. *Christianity Today* magazine summarized the study and offered a snapshot of evangelicalism in America at the beginning of Donald Trump's presidency—a presi-

9. Jake Meador, "American Evangelicalism as a Controversy Generator Machine," *Mere Orthodoxy*, February 6, 2024, https://tinyurl.com/bp9x4epw.

10. Diana Butler Bass, "I Don't Understand," Dianabutlerbass.substack .com, January 25, 2024, https://tinyurl.com/55p5s6cx.

It's Time to Go

dency that placed political and cultural evangelicals center stage: "About a quarter of Americans (26%) are self-identified evangelicals. About two-thirds of those evangelicals are white (64%), while 19 percent are black, 10 percent are Hispanic, and the remaining 6 percent are Asian, mixed race, or other ethnicities."[11] While core beliefs of the faith may be Bebbington-similar in these communities, evangelical expression may look very different in various demographic groups.

Evangelicalism is growing exponentially in other places in our world. At the beginning of 2020, French researcher Sebastian Fath estimated that about 26 percent of the world's 2.5 billion Christians can be classified as evangelical.[12] But the evangelical movement's downsizing in the West illustrates that religious belief and practice are inextricably linked to social, cultural, and political factors.

White evangelical church attendance is in decline in America, according to a 2021 Gallup study: the percentage of White evangelical Protestants fell from 33 percent in 1999 to 21 percent in 2021.[13] Muddying those numbers are people who call themselves evangelicals but do not belong to a local church. Political scientist and statistician Dr. Ryan Burge released a study in 2020 that found that a full 9 percent of self-identified evangelicals do not attend church. (And this figure was before the COVID pandemic upended church and culture around the world; I suspect the numbers would trend higher today.)[14]

---

11. Sarah Eekhoff Zylstra, "1 in 3 American Evangelicals Is a Person of Color," *Christianity Today*, September 6, 2017, https://tinyurl.com/2bjwbb3v.

12. "660 Million Evangelicals in the World?" Evangelical Focus: Europe, February 18, 2020, https://tinyurl.com/rdrat6xt. From the article: Asia has an estimated 215 million evangelical Christians; Africa, 185 million; South America, 123 million; Europe, 23 million; and Oceania has 7 million.

13. Kyle Gray, "The Decline of White Evangelical Protestants," Survey Center on American Life, October 7 2022, https://tinyurl.com/355m2tmy.

14. Ryan P. Burge, "Can You Be an Evangelical and Never Go to Church?" *Religion in Public*, May 18, 2020, https://tinyurl.com/55hj5b4a.

Chapter 1

Professor Daniel K. Williams noted the effect of these disaffiliated people who still view themselves as evangelical: "But without a church community, in many cases, the nation's political system becomes their church—and the results are polarizing. They bring whatever moral and social values they acquired from their church experience and then apply those values in the political sphere with an evangelical zeal."[15]

The expressions of evangelicalism that have flourished in marginalized communities—among the poor, minorities, the disenfranchised, the disabled, and the abused—are the ones who've long learned to travel light, carrying only the essentials with them. Though most of the wild branches within evangelicalism about which I'll be writing are majority White spaces, my own experience as a minority who has experienced antisemitism in some of those White spaces has sensitized me to listen to those at the margins. I hear from those pilgrim voices the values of embracing humility, drawing spiritual strength from community, and above all, clinging to Jesus in a difficult and unjust world.

An Internet meme making the rounds not long ago read, "If Paul saw the church in America, we'd be getting a letter." I understood the sentiment, but my first thought was, "Which church? Which America?"

My own journey through evangelicalism over the last fifty years has shown me that there is no single entity to whom the apostle would address a letter. There are many expressions of evangelicalism.

Are we willing to receive the letters God is sending us, mailed from the margins of the groups and congregations that have formed us? Some of those letters may in fact be mailed from zip codes outside of the evangelical world. Will we simply crumple

---

15. Daniel K. Williams, "What Really Happens When Americans Stop Going to Church," *Atlantic*, September 3, 2023, https://tinyurl.com/a8ad6x6f.

It's Time to Go

those letters and throw them as packing material into the boxes we're sending to the rummage sale?

Before we answer that question, we need to gain clarity on why we're packing in the first place.

Downsizing: Knowing It's Time to Go

When you're ramping up to begin the downsizing process to move from a large house in which you've lived for years, every room crammed full of stuff and memories, the very thought of sifting through it all can be overwhelming. Where do you begin?

After thirteen moves of my own, as well as sorting through the household possessions of a few relatives and friends in order to assist their relocation, I've learned that the necessary first step doesn't require packing a single box. It is coming to terms with the fact that it is time to downsize. It is a little easier to wrap your mind around the necessity of a move into smaller quarters when your reasons are happy ones such as relocating to be near cherished family, or accepting a dream job though it means facing a pricey housing market. But a lot of those facing downsizing do so because of losses or changes in family status. The nest empties. Death or divorce forces sale of a property. Declining health calls for a different kind of living arrangement. Change—even welcome change— carries with it a measure of sorrow as the familiar is uprooted.

Grief is a by-product of downsizing. But so is hope.

The remainder of this book will explore several different but interconnected expressions of evangelicalism that have influenced the movement since it emerged from the Jesus People days. These include parachurch ministries, the Plymouth Brethren, Messianic Judaism, second- and third-wave charismatic renewal, fundamentalism and homeschooling, the church growth movement and the rise of megachurches, spiritual warfare teaching and culture war organizing, and the emergence of or return to formal liturgical forms of worship.

Chapter 1

I recognize there are many, many other kinds of congregations and groups arrayed across the evangelical spectrum, and I hope this book will encourage you to reflect deeply on your own experience. Take an unflinching look at the piles of bulky and nonsensical stuff that may have been deposited in your soul. Your reflection may uncover grief, but I pray that you'll discover the seeds of hope in the process. Recognize that none of us can go back to an earlier time, nor can we stay where we are today. It's time to go. The church is on the move, and we'll need to downsize so we can travel light.

Reflect

1. There is a list at the beginning of this chapter that captures some of the images that come to mind when someone uses the word "evangelical." Which ones most reflect your own experience? Why? What would you add to that list?
2. If you've spent time in an evangelical congregation, how did church leaders and members seem to understand the identity and purpose of both that specific body and the broader (universal) church? If you've been in several congregations over time, what similarities and differences did you witness in how these churches seemed to understand their identity and purpose?
3. Who were the marginalized attending your specific evangelical church community? Who were considered "outsiders" by that community? What sort of letter might these marginalized members or outsiders write to that church community?

2

Who's Going with You?

When I was a child, some of my favorite restaurant dining experiences were at places with a great big buffet. I savored the freedom of being able to bypass the food items I didn't like (vegetables) so I could dine like kid royalty on a meal I selected for myself, which was usually a combination of dinner rolls, fried chicken, and chocolate pudding topped with a mountain of whipped cream and a neon red maraschino cherry. I loved being able to choose from a dizzying array of options—even if I always seemed to end up with fried chicken as my main course.

It was a little like landing at a mile-long spiritual buffet line once I got into the flow of college life in 1977. I was starved for Christian community, and instead of focusing on a single entrée, I piled my plate with just about every option available to me. I sampled everything.

Some of the Christian friends I knew from my hometown had plugged into a campus ministry at Illinois State called Christian Collegians. Christian Collegians hosted frequent Sunday evening dinner gatherings at its Campus House, its headquarters for the ministry located in a worn but beloved old residence not far from

Chapter 2

the edge of the campus. It became my primary fellowship connection but was far from my only one.

After the lonely years listening to sermons on Christian radio alone in my room during high school, I sampled everything else on the buffet including visits to a few Campus Crusade for Christ small-group introductory Bible studies and Intervarsity Christian Fellowship's gatherings, which tended toward more cerebral, issues-focused discussion.

I also sampled spiritually questionable campus ministries. I remember standing among the crowd on campus as traveling evangelist Jed Smock would appear periodically to do a little fire-and-brimstone open-air preaching. He seemed to draw energy from the taunts of the crowd like he was an insult comic, only he was an insult comic who believed every single member of his audience was going to hell. I once sidled up to someone in his entourage and said, *sotto voce*, that I was a believer, too, then immediately felt embarrassed. Was I ashamed of my lack of courage in suffering for Christ by not standing publicly with Jed? Or was I horrified at the scorn he seemed to have for his audience, even those of us who were committed Jesus followers? At the time, I was unsettled for days by both possibilities.

Additional items on my spiritual smorgasbord included visits to a variety of Sunday morning church services ranging from African Methodist Episcopal to Southern Baptist, along with a couple of local Christian Church congregations. I enjoyed each one but was surprised by how formal Sunday morning services could be. People sang a few songs accompanied by a piano or organ, listened to a special musical number performed by a choir or soloist, heard a sermon, passed the plate, and perhaps shared communion, all while sitting in rows that didn't seem all that different than the impersonal lecture halls on campus.

I found the church outside of institutional church services. I recognize that this was in part due to the intense, immersive nature of college life, which was a bubble unlike any other environment most of us would experience once we joined the adult world after graduation. However, also contributing to that sense of community was the Jesus Movement, whose effects still lingered in the Midwest during the late 1970s. There were many new-to-the-faith Jesus freaks like me on campus at that time, on fire with first love for him.

Churched by Parachurch Ministries

Parachurch ministries were responsible for the lion's share of the evangelism and discipleship many of us experienced during our college years. Parachurch ministries are "specialist" Christian organizations that function outside the structure and oversight of a church or denomination. These organizations understand their role as being a complement to the ministry of the local church. Some estimate there are currently more than fifty thousand US-based parachurch ministries.[1] Parachurch organizations often work in partnership with local churches, but their work usually has a specific ministry focus, such as missions, disciple making, relief work, social services, the arts, media, education, publishing, or evangelism.

Parachurch campus groups played a significant role in my first experience of the church. But so did other forms of parachurch ministry. I was catechized by the Jesus music I listened to, created by artists like Love Song, Larry Norman, Randy Stonehill, Nancy Honeytree, the Second Chapter of Acts, and Lamb, who were special favorites of mine because they were Jewish Jesus freaks like me.

---

1. A single figure is hard to come by, as some of these organizations are very small, and others don't specifically identify as Christian. See Christopher P. Scheitle, Erica J. Dollhopf, and John D. McCarthy, "Spiritual Districts: The Origins and Dynamics of US Cities with Unusually High Concentrations of Parachurch Organizations," *Social Science History* 41, no. 3 (2017), https://tinyurl.com/yuyj5z3u; Keith Mathison, "Historical and Theological Foundations," *Ligonier*, August 25, 2014, https://tinyurl.com/yca3p23b.

Chapter 2

I learned about my faith by listening to a radio station that was owned by Moody Bible Institute, a parachurch ministry. The station broadcast lots of sermons, some old-fashioned gospel music, and a few radio dramas like *Unshackled,* which dramatized the conversion stories of the addicts served by another parachurch organization, Pacific Garden Mission. I was tutored by other parachurch television ministries like the *700 Club* and the Billy Graham crusade broadcasts.

I grew spiritually by reading books published primarily by parachurch publishers. I bought those books, along with music, in Christian bookstores. In the mid to late 1970s, the ones I frequented had Jesus Movement names like Logos or the Upper Room, and were run as parachurch ministry centers, offering prayer rooms and Bible studies, in addition to selling Christian merchandise to pay the rent.

I consumed a steady diet of magazines published by parachurch organizations like *Campus Life, Christianity Today,* and the *Wittenburg Door.*[2] But my very favorite periodicals from that time were the underground newspaper *Cornerstone* (published by Jesus People USA) and the urgent prophetic words of the *Last Days Newsletter,* produced by musician Keith Green's Last Days Ministries. Jesus People USA and Last Days were parachurch ministries that emerged directly out of the Jesus Movement.

I learned what it might look like to commit my entire life to Christian service as I got to know a few peers who were in training with the parachurch mission organization Literature Crusades, headquartered at the time in a suburb adjacent to the one in which I grew up.[3] I also got to know students who were enrolled in Chris-

2. *Campus Life* magazine was produced by Youth for Christ before it became part of the *Christianity Today* family of publications in 1982. The magazine's name was changed to *Ignite Your Faith* in 2006 and ceased publication in 2009. "*Ignite Your Faith,*" Wikipedia, last edited May 5, 2024, https://tinyurl.com/ys8x88m8.

3. Literature Crusades changed their name to International Teams in the

Who's Going with You?

tian colleges and Bible schools, and spoke of what it was like to be able to learn with and from other believers. Some of these institutions were connected to historical denominations, but others functioned as parachurch educational ministries. Each of these organizations guided the early steps of my discipleship journey. Evangelicalism wouldn't look or function the way it has without the role of parachurch ministries. In addition, parachurch ministries have given many believers a taste of the kind of community captured by the New Testament word *koinōnia*.

Community 101

Merriam-Webster defines the Greek word *koinōnia* as "intimate spiritual communion and participative sharing in a common religious commitment and spiritual community." The word is used twenty times in the New Testament.[4] *Koinōnia* is categorically different than membership in a bowling league, graduating class, or book club. We humans tend to identify ourselves with people with whom we have some sort of common ground: family, school, circle of friends, employer, an ethnic group, a neighborhood, city, or nation. And though it might seem at first glance that Jesus's followers could be classified as just another affinity group or fan club, *koinōnia* creates a distinctly different, spiritually bonded community from people who might otherwise have nothing in common.

The community that first formed around Jesus comprised people who would likely never have chosen to hang out with one another: adulterers, fishermen, tax collectors, zealots, the oppressed,

---

1980s to move away from the negative association of warfare and forced conversion linked to the word "crusade." The name was changed again more recently to its current iteration, One Collective.

4. See definition and use of *koinōnia* in the Bible at Bible Tools, accessed September 30, 2024, https://tinyurl.com/dz8dcsau.

Chapter 2

those at the margins of society, doubters, and even a handful of those in power, all connected because each one had responded in faith to him.

After Jesus's death, burial, resurrection, and ascension, many Jewish people had poured into Jerusalem, as they did every year, to celebrate the springtime Jewish feast of Shavuot (Pentecost).[5] The Holy Spirit was poured out on those who had gathered for the holy day, and about three thousand people were added to the community of believers on that day. Acts 2:42 describes the nature of this impossible new community: "They devoted themselves to the apostles' teaching and to fellowship, to the breaking of bread and to prayer."[6] The word translated as "fellowship" is *koinōnia*.

The word *koinōnia* isn't always translated as "fellowship" in English, but it is used to describe the committed communion of the Jesus-following community with God and one another (1 Cor. 1:9; 1 John 1:3–7), intimacy with God (Phil. 3:10), a sacrificial financial gift from one part of the community to those in a different city (Rom. 15:26; 2 Cor. 9:13), or welcome and full inclusion of a visiting leader (Gal. 2:9).

I caught glimpses of what *koinōnia* could look like in the parachurch ministries in which I participated. I witnessed sacrificial generosity in community when members of different campus fellowship groups provided weeks of practical medical care for a fellow student so she wouldn't have to drop out of school. I saw a nominally religious friend make a deeper commitment to Christ because of the honest, sacrificial relationships he experienced with other believers that differed significantly from those in the rote religion he'd witnessed during his childhood. *Koinōnia* marked the unique relationships among believers. It is the native tongue of the kingdom of God.

---

5. Lev. 23:16–22.

6. Unless otherwise indicated, all Scripture quotations in this book come from the New International Version (2011).

Who's Going with You?

My college spiritual buffet line might have seemed expansive at the time, but in retrospect I recognize that it was demographically limited. There were few children or people over age forty. While there was a measure of racial diversity, a few students with disabilities, and a mix of urban, suburban, and rural home addresses, by and large, the people with whom I experienced a taste of *koinōnia* were of the same age and life stage as me.

Even so, dining from the buffet of parachurch fellowships during my college years introduced me to the experience of *koinōnia*. It showed me what the church could be.

In the Beginning . . . Parachurch Ministries

But parachurch ministries aren't the church, are they? A quick fly-over of two thousand years of church history offers some intriguing answers to that question.

The New Testament contains accounts of believers gathering locally for worship, teaching, communion, and practical support. At the same time, some of those sharing the gospel found themselves sent to places and people groups with whom they otherwise would have no occasion to visit. The pattern of both local faith communities and traveling teams of missionaries existed in Jewish culture even before the time of Jesus.[7] And after the resurrection of Jesus, traveling bands of believing missionaries worked with local churches but weren't specifically directed by them.[8] They were, in effect, functioning as primitive parachurch organizations.

In the centuries that followed, a prototype of the parachurch movement emerged as small cohorts moved out to the desert and to less-populated areas as a reaction to a church that seemed

---

7. Ralph Winter, "History of the Parachurch," Cru, accessed September 30, 2024, https://tinyurl.com/4fvyv6ws.

8. Jerry White, *The Church and the Parachurch: An Uneasy Marriage* (Portland, OR: Multnomah, 1973), 37.

Chapter 2

to be losing its fire even as it grew in influence, particularly after the emperor Constantine embraced Christianity in AD 312. Those wilderness-bound people weren't trying to create a separate church but to call the church to return to her first love by their example. Over time, the church enfolded much of this monastic movement into its structure.

Five hundred years ago, the rummage sale that birthed Protestantism offered a brand-new vehicle for church reform. However, it only took a few decades before many Protestant groups succumbed to the temptation toward institutionalization. The impulse to "reform the Reformation" emerged in the 1700s, first in Lutheran circles via Pietism. Pietism advocates focused on a personal experience of salvation, discipleship, and Bible reading rather than seeking to reform the church.

Some early Protestant missionary societies emerged from the Pietist spiritual renewal. These missionaries weren't interested in funneling people into a church or denomination as much as they were in introducing people to Jesus. Missiologist Jerry White notes, "It was an unheard-of emphasis to be concerned about ministry to people without bringing them into your fold."[9] This decoupling of mission from enfolding people into the church was a new theological innovation.

Many denominations sent missionaries during this period, but these early nondenominational evangelical missions gave rise during the 1800s to other parachurch service and outreach ministries like the Salvation Army, the Young Men's Christian Association, Moody Bible Institute, and the American Bible Society.

The social and geopolitical shifts of the twentieth century created an environment where spiritual entrepreneurs launched specialized parachurch ministries targeting specific demographic groups within American/Western culture, such as:

9. White, *The Church and the Parachurch*, 47.

Who's Going with You?

- Children—Child Evangelism Fellowship (founded in 1937), Awana (1950)
- Teens—Youth for Christ (1944), Young Life (1941)
- Young adults—InterVarsity Christian Fellowship (1941), Campus Crusade for Christ/Cru (1951)
- Nondenominational adult Bible study—Bible Study Fellowship (1959), Community Bible Study (1971)
- Men—Full Gospel Businessmen's Fellowship (1951)
- Women—Women's Aglow (1967)

By the middle of the century, there was an explosion of other types of specialized parachurch ministries:

- Broadcast ministries—Moody Radio (1926), Christian Broadcasting Network (1960)
- Humanitarian—World Relief (1944), World Vision (1951)
- Short-term missions—Youth with a Mission (1960), Teen Missions International (1970)
- Colleges—Regent University (1968), Liberty University (1970)
- Evangelism—Billy Graham Evangelistic Association (1950), Harvest Crusades (1990)
- Political/cultural education and organization—Moral Majority (1979), Family Research Council (1983)
- Music recording and distribution—Word Records (1951), Integrity Music (1987)
- Sports outreach—Fellowship of Christian Athletes (1954)

Is the proliferation of parachurch ministries an indictment on the failures and shortcomings of local churches? Or perhaps, a reflection on the massive cultural and economic influence of the consumeristic habits of baby boomers? Or were they an expression of a desire for a deeper, more focused commitment to both mission and to other believers that extended beyond the four walls of a local congregation?

Chapter 2

Most evangelicals would affirm that the local church alone has the spiritual authority to offer the sacraments of baptism and communion.[10] Yet outside of those sacraments, parachurch ministries frequently parallel (and sometimes surpass in both quality and emphasis) the kinds of service, learning, prayer, worship, and evangelism that might happen in a local church.

In this era of downsizing, parachurch organizations are facing the same questions that evangelical churches are. In addition, they are dealing directly with specific questions that arise from the work they do and the people they hope to reach. One pointed example of this comes in the realm of cross-cultural missions. Colonialism, the practice of an outside group or nation imposing its culture and government on a people group or nation, was the default setting through much of the history of the modern mission movement. While missionaries sought converts in a region, American and European governments sought power in these same areas, often in tandem with missionaries. Western missionaries often carried the assumption that their culture best reflected the Jesus found in Scripture.

Colonialism and *koinōnia* can't exist in the same space. Most contemporary cross-cultural missionaries now recognize that they must become respectful students of the people they hope to serve. And many mission organizations have repented of their historical roles of setting the agenda in cultures that are not theirs, shifting instead to equipping and supporting local, indigenous church leaders. This offers us a helpful clue as we consider what healthy downsizing might look like.

Some church leaders decry the proliferation of parachurch organizations because they see them as competitors for a limited amount of donor dollars and volunteer time. A few others dismiss parachurch ministries, saying that if the church was doing her job,

10. A rite that is a symbol or sign of a divine reality (Matt. 28:18-20; 1 Cor. 11:23-26).

Who's Going with You?

there would be no need for other kinds of ministries. Both of those stances stifle *koinōnia*.

J. David Schmidt has served many large parachurch ministries for nearly four decades as an organizational consultant.[11] He noted that many parachurch ministries have been born out of a person or group's desire to respond to a need that was not being adequately addressed by a local church or denomination, adding, "The organizational containers we put around God's work are human constructs." He noted that in almost every sector of culture, institutional loyalty is fading fast. The seismic cultural shifts that have emerged in our rising digital age have solidified the reality that we are relating to authority differently than we did a generation ago. Individuals (with help from algorithms) curate information and form relationships according to their preferences, the opinions of their social networks, and sources they've chosen to trust. There is no going back to an earlier time when those old authority structures were in place.

Downsizing: Who's Going with You?

The downsizing process is clarified when you can envision where you're going. If you're moving from a McMansion into a one-bedroom condo, you have a pretty good idea of how much space you will have and can begin thinking strategically about what to get rid of. (The short answer: most of what you own!)

But the spiritual downsizing process doesn't come with a forwarding address. The good news is that it does come with traveling companions who speak the language not of authority but of *koinōnia*, though they might not be the crew we might expect.

We must be willing to interrogate our current practices and comfortable affiliations. Some of the parachurch organizations with whom I've worked in recent years have begun asking a ques-

---

11. Interview, January 3, 2024, with J. David Schmidt of WisePlanning.net.

Chapter 2

tion that cultivates *koinōnia*: "What can we do together that we can't do on our own?"

One illustration of this came out of the efforts of a Chicago-area networking parachurch organization with whom I served. Christ Together Chicago brought local evangelical pastors and church leaders together for prayer, learning, and community outreach.[12] As a result, some meaningful new relationships began to form. In the cradle of those new relationships, some leaders began asking that question. They were willing to wrestle with it and pray together about it.

One of the towns in the area had a high poverty rate. As a result, residents lived in a food desert, an urban area where it was difficult for residents to obtain fresh, wholesome groceries and produce. As a result, in conjunction with neighborhood leaders, some of the congregations in and near the town began dreaming together about creating community gardens in some vacant lots. That effort led to the planting of local produce gardens, but it also grew to include ongoing health and nutrition clinics. The relationships that developed between members of many different churches and people of the community never would have happened if individual churches chose to stay within their respective buildings. It took a parachurch ministry to persist in asking that question and then listen with humility to the people they hoped to serve in the name of Jesus. The partnered churches planted seeds of lettuce and radishes but also sowed seeds of *koinōnia*.

God has wired into each one of us a desire for meaningful spiritual relationship with him and with other believers. The rummage sale happening in evangelicalism does not in any way downsize those God-given desires. Parachurch ministries have played a

---

12. This organization, first known as Catalyst, then as Christ Together Chicago, existed in the northern and northwestern suburbs of Chicago from approximately 2007 to 2013 before shifting its primary focus to evangelism and replicating its efforts in other cities across the United States.

Who's Going with You?

unique role as midwives in the church, facilitating focused mission and birthing *koinōnia* for many. Because of that role, they may well be some of the essential voices that can help us see who is going with us into the future as we sift through the evangelical experience of the last couple of generations in search of *koinōnia*.

Reflect

1. What kinds of parachurch ministries (if any) have influenced your spiritual journey?
2. Do you believe parachurch ministries compete with or complement the ministry of the local church? Why?
3. How does *koinōnia* differ from being in a club or clique? Have you witnessed *koinōnia* in action in any of the faith contexts in which you've worshiped?

3

Assess Your Mess

"I'm sorry. You didn't make the cut."

I got to the end of my sophomore year in college and learned that I wouldn't be permitted to declare a major in my desired subject area. I'd decided to switch from history to deaf education. There were only a few slots open in the deaf education program, as the state of Illinois wanted to ensure that the supply of new teachers met the demand. An administrator told me that though they knew I was a good candidate because they'd seen me working with kids in the classroom, the standard they used to fill the few available spots was grade point average. Mine just wasn't high enough. I was too busy going to campus fellowship activities and church services to have time or energy to net anything close to a 4.0 GPA.

I returned to my parents' home to have a good old-fashioned existential crisis, work for a semester, and try to figure out my next step.[1] Since I was over eighteen, my parents said they would

---

[1] It would be more than thirty years before I entered the classroom again, this time as a seminary student at Northern Seminary outside Chicago.

Assess Your Mess

no longer stop me from attending church, but I was forbidden to talk about my faith in their home. A friend of mine attended a small congregation connected with a Bible school in the area.[2] She invited me to join her at what was dubbed "the Young People's Bible Study," a folksy euphemism for the college and career-age singles group.

I found the group warm and welcoming and soon began attending their Sunday morning church services with my friend. The first time I walked into the school gym where Neighborhood Church met, I noticed many of the women were wearing head coverings—lace doilies pinned to their hair.

None of the churches or fellowship groups I'd visited in college had this unusual dress code. The friend who invited me to the Bible study pointed to 1 Corinthians 11:1–16, which is an extended discussion about men's and women's head coverings in worship. She then shook her long, uncovered tresses and shrugged. "I don't wear one, and no one seems to mind. Don't worry about it."

She let me know that in addition to the head coverings, there were other "Biblical Principles" about how women in the church were supposed to behave. They were to be quiet, modest, simultaneously motherly and virginal, and content to leave the theology and leadership to the men.

I learned these people were Plymouth Brethren, a numerically small group with outsized influence in evangelicalism, though many evangelicals have never heard of them. But if you've heard of the rapture, tried to figure out the identity of the antichrist, read the end-times book series Left Behind, or picked up a *Scofield Ref-*

---

2. The Bible school was connected with a mission organization called Literature Crusades that was run in the early years by Plymouth Brethren missionaries. They changed their name to International Teams during the 1980s in order to distance themselves from the negative historical association with the word "crusade." They rebranded again in 2018 to become One Collective. They're no longer aligned with the Plymouth Brethren.

Chapter 3

erence Bible, you've experienced the theology that originated with the Plymouth Brethren.

And though the notion of "the priesthood of all believers" (see 1 Pet. 2:9) didn't originate with the Plymouth Brethren, that concept is a cornerstone of their self-understanding and approach to corporate worship. Dr. Harry Ironside, pastor of Chicago's Moody Church from 1929 to 1948, observed, "Any real evangelical theologian always milked the Plymouth Brethren cow!"[3]

That cow contributed two different kinds of milk to evangelicalism: dispensationalism and, depending on how you look at it, either a radical return to a first-century form of the church or the Enlightenment-informed enshrining of the individual over the shared life of the congregation.

Charting God's Plan for the Ages

The leaders of Neighborhood Church invited a professor from Dallas Theological Seminary to visit the church each year, who unfurled a giant dispensational chart to explain God's plan for the ages to us.[4] Dispensationalism is a system that describes God's work in time unfolding in a progressive series of seven historical ages, or "dispensations." The first four dispensations covered the revelation of God contained in the Old Testament from Adam to Abraham to Moses to David.

Our current age, the fifth in the series, also known as the Church Age, is a pause or parenthesis in the ongoing march toward the end of days. Dispensationalists generally believe that the Church Age began in Acts 2 and will end when all believers will be instantly and supernaturally removed from the earth (the rapture, referenced

---

3. Quote found in Billy Graham, *Just as I Am* (New York: Harper Collins, 1997), 99.

4. This is similar in nature to the charts explaining dispensationalism that were used at Neighborhood Church: https://tinyurl.com/57d3y9yr.

40

Assess Your Mess

in 1 Thessalonians 4:16–18). The long-paused end-times clock will then resume with a terrible time of testing on the earth, the seven-year Great Tribulation. At the conclusion of this period, a triumphant Jesus will return to earth with the raptured believers to reign for a thousand years over a cleansed, renewed creation. There are varieties of interpretation within dispensationalism that attempt to answer questions like "Will the rapture happen before or during the Great Tribulation?" and "Who is the antichrist?"

In Plymouth Brethren circles, dispensationalism was treated as dogma and spoken of with the same reverence as the virgin birth or the resurrection.

The first time I laid my eyes on that giant chart, I saw that the Jewish people (also known as "God's earthly people," according to the Plymouth Brethren) faced a grim storyline, while Christians ("God's heavenly people") had a much happier one that appeared to include a "Get out of Jail Free" rapture card. I turned to the friend who'd invited me to the church and asked, probably a little too loudly, "As a Jewish believer, exactly where do I fit on that chart?"

She told me I was now in the "Church" category. When I explain to well-meaning gentile Christians that if Adolf Hitler (an antichrist figure if ever there was one!) was rounding up Jews to send them to Auschwitz, he would not care if I confessed that Jesus is my Lord. I'd be in line to the ovens with the rest of my relatives. My faith does not cancel my Jewish identity. It was in that moment, at age nineteen, that I decided I'd better start learning something about theology because the complex yet strangely tidy answers of that dispensational chart left me with lots of questions.

Dispensationalism as we know it did not exist until one of the founders of the Plymouth Brethren movement, ex-Anglican John Nelson Darby, had his own series of revelations in the late 1820s and early 1830s while recovering from a fall from a horse. A couple of outlier characters who lived prior to that time had speculated about some of the components of this system, but no one

41

Chapter 3

at that point had put salvation history together in quite the way Darby did. By the late 1970s, dispensationalism was the de facto understanding not only among the Plymouth Brethren but among a majority of evangelicals. As in, if a person didn't subscribe to dispensationalism, were they a true Christian? I was led to assume they weren't.

The Plymouth Brethren might have invented dispensationalism, but thanks to a series of dispensational Bible conferences in the late 1800s, the publication of the dispensational-influenced *Scofield Reference Bible* in 1909, and the system's adoption by popular Bible teachers like Dwight L. Moody and Lewis Sperry Chafer, it became the default setting for the burgeoning evangelical movement as it flowered throughout the twentieth century. By the time I entered the scene in the 1970s, dispensational theology was everywhere: in the sermons I heard on the Moody Bible Institute radio station, in books like televangelist Ernest Angley's *Raptured* and Hal Lindsey's 1970 blockbuster *The Late Great Planet Earth*, in the 1970 rapture-themed movie *A Thief in the Night*, and in Christian rocker Larry Norman's aching 1969 ballad *I Wish We'd All Been Ready*.

Everyone I knew was certain we were living in the last days, and that the rapture would happen and whisk all the real Christians into the air. I felt I wasn't an especially stellar version of a real Christian. Maybe, then, as a Jewish person I'd be left behind to undergo the Great Tribulation, where the antichrist would be given free rein to rain down every bucket of suffering mentioned in the book of Revelation. My anxiety was high, which was no doubt a sign of my lukewarm faith.

The people of Neighborhood Church weren't taking any chances about the congregation being rapture-ready. We devoted ten weeks of sermon time to view the 1977 film series *How Shall We Then Live?* Theologian and series host Francis Schaeffer led us through the rise and fall of civilizations throughout history, warning us about the urgency of holding the line on conservative social positions. Any form of compromise would push us headfirst down the dreaded "slippery slope," hastening the end of Western civi-

Assess Your Mess

lization. Schaeffer's Reformed theology didn't cloud the message the leaders of Neighborhood Church wanted us to glean from the films, which was "The End is near. Man your battle stations!"

There were other warnings, mostly rumors masquerading as facts, that circulated among the people of Neighborhood Church during those years: devil-worshipers were engaged in widespread ritual child abuse, business conglomerate Procter and Gamble were helping to fund the Church of Satan, Disney movies were created to make witchcraft look fun, and the musicians making secular rock music were implanting secret evil messages in their music.[5] When the rise of QAnon and related conspiracy theories focusing on decoding secret plots and unmasking evil cabals caught fire among evangelicals beginning in 2016–2017, it all felt so familiar. We'd been practicing paranoia in the name of end-times readiness for decades.

Jesus wanted us to be ready for his return (Matt. 24; Luke 21:5–36; John 14:1–4). But the deep anxiety about the end of days among evangelicals immersed in dispensational teaching has resulted in decades of rumormongering and paranoia. This is the fruit that grew from a tree with shallow roots planted in a novel 150-year-old theological system.

Long after I left Neighborhood Church, I learned that for most of Christian history, other views of the end of days were the norm. It was even longer before I could walk into an empty house where I expected there would be people at home, and not have a 10,000-watt jolt of fear that the rapture had taken place and I'd been left behind.[6]

---

5. Satanic ritual abuse: see "Cults That Never Were: The Satanic Ritual Abuse Scare (SRAS)," accessed September 30, 2024, https://tinyurl.com/4xthzhur; Procter and Gamble: Robert Skvarla, "When 1980s Satanic Panic Targeted Procter & Gamble," *Atlas Obscura*, July 13, 2017, https://tinyurl.com/54y5swyu; backmasking: "Backmasking," Wikipedia, last edited September 18, 2024, https://tinyurl.com/2d5xupbz.

6. Rapture anxiety: Kathryn Post, "Rapture Anxiety Is a Thing," *Washington Post*, April 21, 2023, https://tinyurl.com/3f8dr75a. For a helpful overview of the various historical views of the end-times/millennial reign of

Chapter 3

Figs among the Thistles

Though the Plymouth Brethren's dispensationalism emphasized a complicated, coded version of the last days, they also scattered some hopeful seeds in evangelicalism. While they weren't the first Christians to emphasize simplicity in corporate worship gatherings, they did wed that vision of simplicity to their conviction that every believer was called to priestly service.

A typical Sunday morning worship gathering at Neighborhood Church began with a "Spirit-led" selection of hymns and a few accepted contemporary praise songs. Members of the congregation would call out a song number from the hymnal or songbook, and a member who'd had a few years of piano lessons would bang out the accompaniment while we sang every verse. We then moved to testimony time, where members of the congregation would share stories about what God had done in their lives the previous week. These testimonies tended to focus either on opportunities to share the gospel or thanksgiving for God's care in a trial. Next came an expository message on a passage of Scripture by one of the elders before we moved into weekly communion, which they called "the breaking of bread." It was, quite literally, the breaking of a huge, yeasty loaf of white bread into chunks shared only by those who'd made a profession of faith in Christ, accompanied by a swig from a cup of unfermented grape juice.

There was a team of elders running Neighborhood Church. "The Bible doesn't say anything about a pastor," more than one person told me. "We do what the Bible says, and it talks throughout the New Testament about elders overseeing the local church. We're a New Testament church."

I heard the phrase "the priesthood of all believers" frequently. It was used to remind us that no one could outsource our spiritual

---

Christ, see "Survey of Eschatological Views," Bible.org, accessed September 30, 2024, https://tinyurl.com/yf33cywn.

Assess Your Mess

lives to others. There were sideswiped little barbs contrasting our church full of priests with either the Catholic Church, with their pomp and religious hierarchy, or the lukewarm mainliners, who didn't take the gospel seriously like *we* did.

I also gleaned from the way the words were used at church that this phrase meant each individual Christian had religious authority and autonomy, at least in theory. The emphasis in those circles was on the "priesthood" part . . . and not so much on "all believers." I noticed that the men of the church used the phrase often. The women rarely did.

The reclamation of the notion of the priesthood of all believers didn't originate with the Plymouth Brethren. It is rooted in God's calling of Israel as his chosen people: "Now if you obey me fully and keep my covenant, then out of all nations you will be my treasured possession. Although the whole earth is mine, you will be for me a kingdom of priests and a holy nation" (Exod. 19:5-6a).

This calling for all of Israel to be a kingdom of priests was distinct from the specific priestly role God gave to the tribe of Levi, who was set apart from the rest of the people to serve in the tabernacle, teach the law, and function as judges (Num. 3:40-51; Num. 18; Deut. 17:8-13; 33:8-11). Rabbinic scholar Nissan Dovid Dubov explains what it means to be chosen to be a kingdom of priests: "The priest's function is to 'bring' G-d to the people, and to elevate the people to be nearer to G-d. The purpose of the Jews is to bring G-d to the world and the world closer to G-d."[7] A priest was tasked with the privilege of reflecting God's light to others through worship, intercession, instruction, and service. God called each member of the chosen people from youngest to oldest, male and female alike, for this mission to the rest of the world.

---

7. Nissan Dovid Dubov, "The Chosen People: Chosen for What?" Chabad.org, accessed September 27, 2024, https://tinyurl.com/3d7b9m58, spelling theirs: observant Jews write God's name without the vowel as a sign of respect for his holiness.

Chapter 3

Jesus's first-century Jewish followers would have understood through the lens of their heritage the language Peter used: "But you are a chosen people, a royal priesthood, a holy nation, God's special possession, that you may declare the praises of him who called you out of darkness into his wonderful light" (1 Pet. 2:9). The writer of Hebrews uses chapters 4–10 to highlight the goodness, finality, and superiority of Jesus's high priesthood. Revelation 1:6 identifies the followers of Christ as "a kingdom and priests to serve his God and Father." Jesus's followers were meant to live out the calling first given to the chosen people to serve as priests to the world.

However, as the church gained legitimacy, power, and wealth over the following centuries, religious leaders adopted distinctly different roles from those of laypeople, mirroring the structure of civil governments across Europe. Amid the other ways in which the spiritually renewed monk Martin Luther challenged the religious power structures of his day was his revelation that Scripture told believers they didn't need to rely on a cleric to come to God on their behalf. Their faith in Jesus saved them and freed them to serve him in grateful response. Though Luther hoped to call the Catholic Church to repentance, they excommunicated him— tossed to the curb like yesterday's trash—in 1521.

Despite this, Luther's message caught fire and was a part of the wave of spiritual housecleaning sweeping through Europe's churches. This Protestant re-formation began to shrink the canyon dividing professional clergy from laity, thanks in part to the recovery and embrace of the Bible's language of "priesthood of all believers."

Even as the gulf narrowed, a new chasm formed. Baked into the DNA of Protestantism was a readiness to divide from other believers. Some estimates suggest that there are now more than forty-five thousand different Protestant denominations worldwide. Perhaps most startling is that the people doing the analysis counted the many independent, nondenominational churches as one "denomination" for statistical purposes.[8] Just imagine what the figure would be if each independent congregation was counted as its own denomination.

While many churches are launched in response to a deep sense of mission, a sizable percentage of new churches are created as a reaction to the issues or problems from the last congregation to which a church planter belonged. The priesthood of all believers sometimes has been interpreted to mean, "Hey, Pastor, you're not the boss of me!"

I witnessed the effects of this priestly propensity to divide at Neighborhood Church. I was too young and new to the world of the Plymouth Brethren to recognize the fault lines that existed in this small congregation of about 80 to 100 people. One Sunday, a few regulars didn't appear. The next week, a few more were absent. Over the next couple of months, a handful of others joined them. "They felt called to join a different congregation," someone explained to me.

All of them? At once?

As a result of that first exodus, another clique departed. Eventually, the small group that remained at Neighborhood Church decided it was time to disband.

The church had given me one remarkable gift—my husband, Bill, whom I met at the Young People's Bible Study. We were both new in our faith and were confused by the experience of attending a church that was undergoing a split. It seemed every priest in the place was exerting their own authority.

Not long ago, I reached out to a couple of people who were a part of the congregation to find out if they remembered what caused the division. No one could.

Humorist and storyteller Garrison Keillor grew up Plymouth Brethren. In his 1985 book *Lake Wobegon Days*, he cap-

---

8. "How Do You Define a Denomination?," Center for the Study of Global Christianity at Gordon-Conwell Theological Seminary, accessed September 27, 2024, https://tinyurl.com/yupzes2.

Chapter 3

tured the propensity for division that existed from the beginning among them:

> The first Brethren . . . left the Anglican church in 1865 to worship on the basis of correct principles . . . unified in their opposition to the pomp and corruption of the Christian aristocracy.
>
> Unfortunately, once they were free of the worldly Anglicans, these firebrands were not content to worship in peace but turned their guns on each other. Scholarly to the core and perfect literalists every one, they set to arguments that, to any outsider, would have seemed very minor indeed but which to them, were crucial to the Faith, including the question: if Believer A is associated with Believer B who has somehow associated himself with C, who holds a False Doctrine, must D break off association with A, even though A does not hold the doctrine, to avoid the taint?
>
> The correct answer is: Yes. Some Brethren, however, felt that D should only speak with A and urge him to break off with B. The Brethren who felt otherwise promptly broke up with them.
>
> Once having tasted the pleasure of Being Correct and Defending True Doctrine, they kept right on and broke up at every opportunity, until, by the time I came along, there were dozens of tiny Brethren groups, none of which were speaking to the others.[9]

Downsizing: Assess Your Mess

Downsizing of a physical space requires a hard-nosed approach to evaluating the possessions you've accumulated. There are items that may have once seemed to serve a purpose (the dangerous 1960s lawn dart game tucked into the corner of a garage or the

9. Garrison Keillor, *Lake Wobegon Days* (New York: Viking, 1985), 105-6.

1990s bread machine collecting dust in a cabinet) but were little more than novelties with no lasting value.

Spiritual downsizing calls for the kind of discernment that can assess with wisdom the lasting consequences of spiritual novelty acts and rediscovered faith practices.

Two thousand years of Christian history is full of stories of theological innovations like Arianism or Nestorianism that were popular for a time before being discarded by those holding the line on theological orthodoxy. I've seen more evangelical academic leaders interrogating dispensationalism's theological innovations or moving away from dispensationalism entirely in recent years, though it still has a grip on the imaginations and politics of many evangelical churchgoers. Will dispensationalism lose that hold as a downsized church moves into the future? And if so, what might the church look like without it as it responds to current events? These are conversations worth having as we sort through evangelicalism's recent past.

The Plymouth Brethren didn't invent simple church gatherings governed by a plurality of elders rather than a single lead pastor, nor are they the only ones in evangelicalism who order their congregations in this way. Though the system at Neighborhood Church had some mysterious issues lurking under the surface that led to the congregation's demise, the relatively flat hierarchy had some things going for it that may speak to the future of a downsized church: simplicity in structure, cultivation of many apt preachers and teachers rather than relying on a single master communicator pastor, and a desire for collaboration in governance.

The Plymouth Brethren also took seriously the notion of all believers being priests, though it was applied differently in those circles to men and women. (We will be taking a closer look at gender roles in evangelicalism in chapter 7.) Sometimes the language of "the priesthood of all believers" has been used to justify an individual's preferences, rather than focusing on what it meant to serve in that role. However, the man usually credited with bringing

Chapter 3

the phrase to the fore during the last rummage sale in the church, Martin Luther, said, "The priest is not made. He must be born a priest; must inherit his office. I refer to the new birth—the birth of water and the Spirit. Thus all Christians must became priests, children of God and co-heirs with Christ the Most High Priest." He went on to note that while most people liked the title of priest, they didn't embrace the sacrificial nature of the role: "The Christian priesthood costs life, property, honor, friends and all worldly things. It cost Christ the same on the holy cross."[10]

A downsized church may be a tool God will use to expose unhealthy motivations like playing the "priesthood of all believers" card in the name of personal preference. Of course, we have also moved into an era where it is easier than ever to curate our own church experience online through a combination of streamed worship services, podcasts featuring favorite preachers, and online affinity groups and Bible studies. A smaller evangelicalism will condense our choices, but it will take the work of the Spirit doing what only he can do to recalibrate evangelicals to learn to live in terms of "we," not "me," and to lay aside the privilege we claim from priesthood so we are free to serve God and others.

Reflect

1. If you have been a part of evangelicalism at any point during the last fifty years, you've likely been exposed to—or perhaps even immersed in—the dispensational view of the last days. How has this view shaped your faith?
2. Is the idea of a barebones, organic weekly worship service too idealistic or dismissive of two thousand years of church history and tradition? Why?
3. Is the phrase "the priesthood of all believers" familiar to you

10. Martin Luther, "First Sunday after Epiphany," in *Complete Sermons of Martin Luther*, vol. 4 (Grand Rapids: Baker Books, 2007), 9.

Assess Your Mess

based on the church circles in which you've traveled? If the phrase itself isn't familiar, have you seen either of the concepts outlined in this chapter (spiritual authority granted to individual believers, followers of Christ representing him to the world) highlighted in your church community?

4

Commit to Purposeful Pruning

When I got engaged to Bill a few months after we started dating, my parents were less than enthusiastic. He was an intelligent, hardworking guy, and his mom was Jewish, which meant that most rabbis considered him Jewish.[1] My mom and dad weren't upset that I'd put my college plans on hold. They weren't upset that I was only nineteen years old, and that Bill and I had dated for a very short time.

They were upset because I'd met him at Neighborhood Church.

Bill's gentile father and Jewish mother had attended a Unitarian church sporadically while they were raising their kids, which seemed like the ideal interfaith solution to their mixed-religion household. During his senior year of high school, Bill discovered a *Steps to Peace with God* tract produced by the Billy Graham Evangelistic Association that his mother had tossed on their dining room table after she'd visited a community Bible study. The tract piqued his curiosity, so he picked up a Bible, read the Gospel

---

1. "Who Is a Jew: Matrilineal Descent," My Jewish Learning, accessed September 27, 2024, https://tinyurl.com/kamtd5wv.

Commit to Purposeful Pruning

of Matthew in three days, and committed his life to Christ when he finished reading. He found his way to Neighborhood Church, where some of the leaders took him under their wing and began to disciple him.

He had always treasured his Jewish heritage and longed to know more about it now that he was a follower of the Jewish Jesus. Marrying me seemed to solidify that for him, even though our wedding was preceded by a complicated, tense series of negotiations with my parents. Though not especially observant, they told us they refused to attend a wedding ceremony on the Jewish Sabbath. My family's usual Shabbat observance almost always included a Saturday morning trip to the beauty salon for my mom and yard work for my dad. They also emphasized they didn't want the ceremony to be too "Christian."

I knew we'd regret it later if my family boycotted the day, so in the end, we landed on a series of compromises with my parents that managed to please no one. They agreed that since they didn't have a rabbi in mind to perform the ceremony, one of the elders from Neighborhood Church could perform the ceremony as long as he was willing to tone down the Jesus talk. In exchange, my parents could control the rest of the wedding day. Despite their lukewarm feelings about the groom, they viewed a big event like this as their opportunity to repay the various invitations to weddings and bar mitzvahs they had received over the years. They were determined to have a fancy affair. They hired a wedding planner, rented event space, and secured a band. I don't remember being asked for my opinion on much of it, though it is possible they may have asked. I didn't really care. Bill's family shrugged off most of the drama and stoically did what was required of them that day.

I treasure two moments from the wedding: the exchange of our vows, and a moment during the reception when the band struck up the Jewish folk song "Hava Nagila" and everyone, including our small contingent of Plymouth Brethren guests, joined to dance the traditional hora. The rest of the day was a tense blur.

53

Chapter 4

It was a relief to make our exit toward the end of the Sunday afternoon reception.

And Now for Something Completely Different

After the wedding, my parents went back to keeping us at arm's length. Nevertheless, Bill and I were full of young newlywed optimism about our future. Our first reality check came a few months after our wedding when Neighborhood Church began its messy dissolution just as I was learning the kinds of Christian subculture things that seemed as familiar as an old sweatshirt to everyone else, from how to celebrate Christian holidays to recipes suitable for a church potluck. I was an eager student but also quietly struggled with the implication that to be a follower of Jesus might mean forgetting who I was. Bill, on the other hand, was realizing that his functionally agnostic upbringing had muted his own Jewish heritage.

We launched our search for a new faith community in a completely different direction from the rest of those who'd scattered from Neighborhood Church. We visited a young Messianic congregation called B'nai Maccabim (Children of the Maccabees).[2] A Messianic congregation anchors itself in the Jewishness of the gospel, though we would soon discover that these small congregations were far from uniform in their approaches to practice, liturgy, and relationships with both the Jewish community and the church.

B'nai Maccabim was a group of from thirty to forty people who gathered for Friday evening Kabbalat Shabbat (Welcoming the Sabbath) services. The congregation comprised young Jewish

2. The Maccabees were a small group of Hebrew zealots who reclaimed the temple in Jerusalem from Seleucid/Greek control in 164 BC. The Jewish holiday of Chanukah commemorates this improbable victory, and the restoration of the temple to worship of God.

54

Commit to Purposeful Pruning

professionals and a handful of Messianic-curious gentiles. The services included some traditional prayers in Hebrew, many of which felt as familiar to me as my own DNA, sung worship that included Scripture set to Jewish-flavored melody and contemporary praise songs written by other young Jewish followers of Jesus. The sermons were given by a rotating cast of teachers, similar to what we'd experienced at Neighborhood Church. It was comforting to be among others who had experienced hostility from both their families and the larger Jewish community because of their faith in Jesus.

Shortly after our daughter was born in 1983, we began attending a more established Messianic congregation that offered child care during services. Adat Hatikvah (Congregation of the Hope) had been in existence since 1934. It was first known as the Chicago Hebrew Christian Church before changing its name to Adat Hatikvah in 1974. The congregation had a spiritual leader with deep Jewish roots who had also served as an adjunct faculty member for a time at a nearby evangelical college.

After I discovered I was expecting our second child in 1985, we rented an apartment closer to my husband's workplace and discovered what was billed as a small Messianic congregation meeting near our new home. But this gathering was quite different in tone and focus: it held a Sunday morning church service with an occasional Messianic song and a few Yiddish phrases thrown into the sermons. The congregation was composed almost entirely of gentiles who had come from a nearby nondenominational Bible church to plant a Hebrew-flavored daughter congregation as an evangelistic outreach in an area with a growing Jewish population.[3] During our year at this congregation, we were treated

---

3. A Bible church "profess(es) to adhere to the Bible as their standard of faith and practice. However, they are of no particular Christian denomination (non-denominational), so there is no formal prescribed belief system to govern them." From "What Is a Bible Church?," Got Questions, accessed October 1, 2024, https://tinyurl.com/d88fjsch. Some but not all

Chapter 4

like trophies ("Lookee here! We got us some Jewish people in our flock!") or projects ("Jewish people like you are the targets of our ministry!"). It was almost as though we were being grafted into a gentile olive tree, which was an odd inversion of the way the apostle Paul spoke of his own Jewish people in Romans 11.

Cultivating Wild Branches: A Brief History

It would be easy to dismiss the effect the numerically small Messianic movement has had on evangelicalism. After all, Jewish people constitute .02 percent of the world's population, and educated estimates place the number of Jewish followers of Jesus worldwide between 100,000 and 300,000.[4] However, the Messianic movement has had outsized influence in evangelicalism during the last fifty years, sparking the beginnings of a long-overdue theological reckoning in the majority-gentile church with what it means to be grafted into an already-existing olive tree, and enmeshment in right-wing political engagement related to the modern nation of Israel.

When Paul told the church in Rome that the gospel was for all, "first to the Jew, then to the Gentile" (Rom. 1:16), he was affirming the way the gospel came to the world, as well as describing his own priorities in mission.[5] Paul's masterful metaphor describing Jesus's family tree of faith in Romans 11 highlighted the gracious way in which God had ingrafted gentiles through faith into his covenant with the Jewish people. He noted that some of the natural-born branches of this olive tree had been broken off, and wild olive

---

Bible churches belong to fellowships of like-minded congregations such as the Independent Fundamental Churches of America.

4. David Lazarus, "Messianic Jews in the World Today," *Israel Today*, April 20, 2021, https://tinyurl.com/23nc9t65.

5. For a helpful extended discussion of this passage and its implications for mission, see "To the Jew First," Gateway Center for Israel, accessed October 1, 2024, https://tinyurl.com/yc58zjx6.

Commit to Purposeful Pruning

branches representing the gentiles had been grafted onto the tree in their place (Rom. 11:17). He warned the ingrafted gentiles not to allow pride to blind them to the reality that God could return those branches he'd removed back to their home on the olive tree (Rom. 11:18–21). Paul wanted them to understand that the hardness of heart toward Jesus among many in the Jewish community of his day was not a surprise to God. Instead, Paul hoped his gentile siblings in faith would recognize that this hardening of Jewish hearts was grace to the gentiles. It unfolded against the unchanging backdrop of God's irrevocable covenant with the chosen people (Jer. 33:25–26).

By the beginning of the third century AD, Jews had become a minority in the church. The combination of antisemitic teaching from some prominent church fathers and great hostility from nonbelieving Jewish leaders toward Jewish believers drove the small remnant underground.[6] Concurrent to this, and continuing to this day, the Jewish people have experienced persecution, expulsion, confiscation of their property, and forced "conversion" to state-run Christianity. Despite these horrors, a miraculous, tiny trickle of born-again Jewish believers has flowed into the church in every century.[7]

The rise of the modern mission movement in the 1800s changed the approach to Jewish evangelism. Those with evangel-

---

6. An excellent scholarly exploration of the Jewishness of the early church can be found in Oskar Skarsaune's *In the Shadow of the Temple: Jewish Influences on Early Christianity* (Downers Grove, IL: InterVarsity Press, 2002). For additional perspective on the topic, this interview with professor of Jewish studies Pieter van der Horst offers a provocative analysis of antisemitism in the early church: "The Origins of Christian Anti-Semitism: Interview with Pieter van der Horst," Jerusalem Center for Security and Foreign Affairs (JCFA), May 5, 2009, https://tinyurl.com/2cbmxmtd.

7. For a helpful overview of the Messianic movement's place in church history: "Messianic Jews: A Brief History," Jews for Jesus, July 21, 2014, https://tinyurl.com/4w2h5jes.

Chapter 4

ical sensibilities didn't view the Jewish people as Christ-killers, as had been the default setting in the church for centuries, but as a unique group of people in need of good news.[8] Suffice it to say, the mainstream Jewish community did not see this as much of an improvement over previous eras in their relations with the church. In the eyes of most Jewish people, evangelism was just another form of identity-erasing antisemitism.

Out of early evangelical mission efforts, a few Hebrew Christian churches (including the forebear congregation to Adat Hatikvah) emerged in urban centers in Europe and the United States, though most new Jewish believers ended up becoming members of already-existing churches and denominations. These Hebrew Christian churches were a first attempt to contextualize the gospel for those who'd come from Jewish backgrounds.[9]

Jewish ministry would change shape because of two nearly simultaneous events: Israel's astonishing victory in the 1967 Six Day War and the Jesus Movement, which had its beginnings in 1969.

---

8. Mission enterprises that began during those years and continue (usually under different names today) include Britain's Anglican London Society for Promoting Christianity amongst the Jews (founded in 1809), now known as the Church's Ministry to the Jews, and the Hebrew Christian Alliance (1860). In America, the Brownville Mission to the Jews (1894), which is now Chosen People Ministries; the Hebrew Christian Alliance of America (1915), now known as the Messianic Jewish Alliance of America; and the Chicago Hebrew Mission, now known as Life in Messiah International (1887).

9. Missiologist Howard Culbertson of Southern Nazarene University defined contextualization as: (1) The process of connecting biblical revelation to a specific culture in a way that the gospel can be understood and lived out in culturally meaningful ways. (2) Based on the premise that people can follow Jesus while maintaining their ethnic or cultural identity. (3) Involves not only the wording of theological expressions but also tangible aspects of church life such as music, artwork, and leadership selection. (4) Enables the gospel to be offensive to each culture for exactly the right reasons and engages people at the level of their deepest needs. https://tinyurl.com/3h 6fpce3, accessed January 20, 2024.

Commit to Purposeful Pruning

Young Jewish believers felt empowered to create communities that reflected their own culture and history. These new congregations were characterized by their commitment to resisting assimilation and the loss of Jewish identity that had been a historical pattern among those who'd come to faith in earlier generations.

A writer for the Gateway Center for Israel, an evangelical organization supportive of Messianic Judaism, affirmed that the Messianic movement is rooted in questions of identity: "One of the centermost claims at the heart of the Messianic movement is that *Jewish identity matters*. If 'Christian' identity was all that mattered, there would be no need for a separate movement. Messianic Jewish congregations came into existence partly as a result of the difficulty of maintaining Jewish identity *within* the typical Christian church."[10]

There was nothing resembling a consensus among the various missionary organizations committed to sharing the gospel with the Jewish people about what kind of congregational setting would be best for the many new believers coming to faith. We'd discovered those tensions in the three congregations we attended in the early 1980s.[11]

---

10. "Messianic Judaism: Perspective Paper," Gateway Center for Israel, accessed October 1, 2024, https://tinyurl.com/nheedamk.

11. The primary umbrella organization for US Jewish-centric churches was the Hebrew Christian Alliance of America, which was formed in 1915 to unite a variety of earlier Protestant mission outreaches to the Jewish people. The nomenclature ("Hebrew Christian") pointed to the church-centric focus of the organization. The Alliance changed its name in 1975 to the Messianic Jewish Alliance of America (MJAA) to reflect the emerging shift toward a Messianic Jewish organizational identity. Other emerging Messianic Jewish leaders who believed their congregations needed to root themselves firmly in practices informed by traditional rabbinic Judaism broke in 1979 from the MJAA to form the Union of Messianic Jewish Congregations (UMJC). Though the MJAA and the UMJC underwent a formal reconciliation process in the 1990s, the two organizations continue to operate separately, holding separate conferences and ministry focuses. There

Chapter 4

The evangelistic efforts of parachurch organizations like Chosen People Ministries and Jews for Jesus, combined with the growth in the number of Messianic congregations, drew the anger of the mainstream Jewish community. Jewish believers were accused of syncretization, the effort to try to blend two disparate faiths into something new, and cultural appropriation, where those of one faith borrow symbols or rituals from another faith or culture, then use it/them thoughtlessly or disrespectfully for their own purposes.[12] A 2016 Pew Research Survey found that only 34 percent of American Jews consider Messianic Jews members of the Jewish community.[13]

Many in evangelical congregations had questions of their own about Messianic Judaism. Some asked whether this movement was just a version of modern-day "Judaizers" teaching justification by works and adopting Jewish religious practices.[14] Some evangelicals wondered aloud why those in congregations that took

---

are some congregations that maintain membership in both organizations, but most have chosen one or the other. As of this writing in 2023, the MJAA counts 154 congregations worldwide in their member roll, and the UMJC has 75. There are an estimated 100,000 Messianic Jews and an additional 200,000 partly Jewish or gentile family members or friends who attend these congregations, per "Messianic Jews in the World Today," *Israel Today*, accessed October 1, 2024, https://tinyurl.com/5d62nrz7.

12. A sampling of those concerns: Hadara Graubart, "Messianic Jews Are Different," *Tablet*, June 18, 2009, https://tinyurl.com/45rxyrx5; Tamar Fox, "Who Are Messianic 'Jews'?" My Jewish Learning, accessed October 1, 2024, https://tinyurl.com/3usknky3; Alissa Wilkinson, "Why Christians Keep Appropriating Jewish Ritual Symbols," *Vox*, January 15, 2021, https://tinyurl.com/yuu4wxv7; Hillary Kaell, "Pastors Wrapped in Torah: Why So Many Christians Are Appropriating Jewish Ritual," *Forward*, October 18, 2020, https://tinyurl.com/4jaduaha.

13. "People of Jewish Background and Jewish Affinity," Pew Research Center, May 11, 2021, https://tinyurl.com/mryzmd9h.

14. The term comes from Gal. 2:14, where Paul confronts Peter about his hypocrisy in asking gentiles to observe Jewish customs in order to become a part of the body of Christ.

Commit to Purposeful Pruning

their cues from traditional Jewish worship practices and described themselves as "Messianic Jews" didn't just call themselves Christians if they believed in Jesus.

By the 1990s, Messianic congregations were drawing larger numbers of gentiles. Some were those burned or burned out by their evangelical church experience and in search of something different. Others had developed an interest in the Hebrew roots of Christianity. With the advent of the Internet, there was no shortage of people who'd set up their own "Hebrew Roots" ministries. Some of these were theologically sound, and many others were flat-out wacky or heretical.

Even after we no longer worshiped in a Messianic congregation, Bill and I continued to stay connected to the Messianic world via occasional visits and our involvement with a discipleship ministry based in Jerusalem. Between 2015 and 2019, however, Bill and I lived near the place where Adat Hatikvah was meeting. We attended the congregation during that time, but it felt a little bit like Rip Van Winkle waking up after his years' long nap in a world that was at once familiar and completely different. There were a handful of faces we remembered from the past, but most of the congregation was now composed of gentiles who'd chosen to worship in a Jewish context.

Theological Questions, Political Activism

We discovered through the years that many gentiles were drawn to Messianic congregations in search of a fresh start after an experience of church hurt or spiritual abuse. Others had theological questions or social/political convictions that weren't being addressed adequately in evangelical spaces. Those questions and convictions have spilled into evangelicalism far beyond the boundary lines of the Messianic Jewish world.

Theology: For most of Christian history, supersessionism, or replacement theology, has been the default setting when it comes to

Chapter 4

the Old Testament and the Jewish people. Supersessionism teaches that the church has superseded (replaced) Israel as God's covenantal, chosen people. Replacement theology asserts that Christians are now God's true Israel, and all of God's promises to Israel now belong to the church. Replacement theology has been weaponized against the Jewish people by figures ranging from early church fathers like Justin Martyr to Reformation hero Martin Luther to modern-day mass murderer Adolf Hitler. Supersessionism has left in its wake generations of trauma, loss, and upheaval among my people.

It has also left the church disconnected from her Romans 11 roots. As a result, the predominant view in the church has often been that the God of the Old Testament is different in personality and character from the God portrayed by the New Testament. Thus, much of the Old Testament functions as nothing more than a very long and sometimes puzzling introduction to the "real" story of the Bible.

While dispensationalism might seem at first to be an alternative to replacement theology, it also communicates that the church has replaced Israel in the current dispensation, while tokenizing the Jewish people by treating them as "God's end-times timepiece." The popularity of dispensationalism in the evangelical world has led to the rise of Christian Zionism, or support for the Jewish people to inhabit their ancient homeland. This idea first took root among British Anglicans in the mid-1800s. This provided inspiration and funding to Jewish Zionists, who had already been working toward this goal. (We'll be exploring Christian Zionism a bit further in chapter 9.)

Politics: Most evangelical dispensationalists as well as some from other streams of Protestantism saw the founding of the modern state of Israel in 1948 as a partial fulfillment of biblical prophecy. "God's end-times timepiece" was now tick-tick-ticking. The rise of Christian Zionism may have been fueled by dispensational theology, but it had political implications. Prominent evangelical leaders associated with Christian Zionism include Jerry Falwell, Pat Robert-

Commit to Purposeful Pruning

son, Hal Lindsey, and John Hagee, whose organization, Christians United for Israel, has been a dominant voice for more than two decades in both prayer and political lobbying efforts. Apocalyptic Christian Zionism rooted in dispensationalism has become a significant influence in America's Middle Eastern foreign policy.[15]

There has been vociferous pushback against the conservative dispensational approach to Middle Eastern politics from some younger or more progressive evangelicals. The anti-Zionist rhetoric coming from this flank of the church characterizing the Israeli people as genocidal colonizers (or Nazis!) is a reaction to Christian Zionism's influence on international politics. Christian Zionism frequently tokenizes the history and identity of the Jewish people, while anti-Zionism often becomes full-blown antisemitism.

Messianic Judaism is numerically insignificant in the wild world of evangelicalism, and not all Messianic Jews even identify themselves as part of that movement. The Messianic community not only represents the beginnings of the church two thousand years ago but continues to influence the majority gentile church to this day in profound ways far beyond its size. It also may offer a hopeful message about the downsizing we are currently experiencing.

Downsizing: Commit to Purposeful Pruning

The metaphor of the olive tree is a potent clarifier of the relationship of Jewish and gentile followers of Jesus in the church. Like

---

15. There has been a rise in criticism of the way Christian Zionism has affected US foreign policy. A sampling of this criticism includes: William N. Dale, "The Impact of Christian Zionism on American Policy," *American Diplomacy* 9, no. 2 (2004), https://tinyurl.com/snc59au2; "Factsheet: Christian Zionism," Religion Media Centre, accessed October 1, 2024, https://tinyurl.com/zaa9ywfy; Tiffany Stanley, "Crowded GOP Field Vies for the Christian Zionist Vote as Israel's Rightward Shift Spurs Protests," Associated Press, July 18, 2023, https://tinyurl.com/yc6bwacy.

Chapter 4

the many other agricultural images used throughout Scripture, it underscores the relationship of creation to its Creator. The single olive tree to which Paul referred in Romans 11 is cultivated by the Master Gardener's pruning (John 15:2). His cropping and lopping remove the deadwood that drains vitality from the tree so it will bear good fruit. In this era of downsizing, the olive tree tells us a profound story about both our faith identity and the reality that God is at work pruning when we find ourselves living through the seismic shift of a giant spiritual rummage sale. After all, what is pruning but purposeful downsizing?

It has been helpful to me to think of my own physical downsizing and relocation experiences over the years first in terms of selective pruning rather than wholesale annihilation. This orientation helped me to commit wholeheartedly in what was sometimes a difficult process by recognizing that God holds the pruning shears, and that pruning creates space for healthy growth.

The olive tree is facing pruning. For every biblically sound Messianic congregation and Hebrew roots ministry, many others are heterodox in theology or practice. This isn't limited to Messianic Judaism, of course. We see it in every stream of the church, but I find myself amazed at the proliferation of Messianic "experts" that have set up shop online in recent years hawking their insights and looking for followers. If there is anything positive to say about this, it is that some of this wacky stuff points to a genuine hunger among some believers to learn about the foundations of their faith. Mature discernment among those hungry believers will lead to pruning wacky teaching and steering clear of the combative character of those Internet teachers who insist that they have special insight and the rest of the church is always 100 percent wrong.

Most Jewish believers I've known believe we have a unique role in offering our gentile evangelical siblings desperately needed insight into how theology and contemporary politics have real-world consequences for the Jewish community. In addition, pruned and growing Messianic Judaism can provide the kind of

Commit to Purposeful Pruning

bridge-building education that helps the wider church live into the seamless relationship between the Old Testament and the New. When evangelicals together with their Messianic siblings in faith can soberly assess the past, repent of theological errors and faith practices, and give and receive forgiveness, natural and ingrafted branches will flourish together.

Reflect

1. Have you had experience with the Messianic Jewish community? If so, what were your impressions? If not, what questions did this chapter's information spark in you about the movement?

2. Have you witnessed the effect of evangelical theological convictions about the role of the modern state of Israel and Christian Zionism in a local congregation? If so, in what way(s)?

3. What can you glean from the apostle Paul's words in Romans 11 about how God ingrafts into his family tree and why and when he elects to prune that tree? How might those insights shape your understanding of the downsizing process?

5

Grief Is a Part of the Process

In 1986, Bill and I had outgrown our small apartment with two children aged two and under, and another baby on the way. A small inheritance gave us enough money for a down payment on a townhome nearly an hour's drive from our small apartment. We relocated to a far-flung exurb of Chicago whose main claim to fame was that the bowling alley in the middle of town was used as a money-laundering business by the mafia.

There was no Messianic congregation near our new home, so we began searching for a church. Our sister-in-law told us she knew of a nearby church that some of her friends attended. When we went to visit, we received a warm welcome from the young, high-energy group at Northwest Suburban Fellowship.[1] The church had one marked difference from our previous congregations. The singing was punctuated every so often by someone offering a message in an otherworldly, unknown language, usually (but not always) followed by an interpretation in English, or a "prophetic word," which was most often a verse or two of

---

1. The church name and the names of church leaders have been changed.

Grief Is a Part of the Process

Scripture, or a message like "God loves this church so much. We are the apple of his eye."

Though Bill and I met at a church that believed that "sign gifts" like speaking in unknown tongues, interpretation, miracles, and words of prophetic insight ceased to exist after the closing of the New Testament canon, we didn't share that conviction. We were children of the Jesus Movement and had experienced God's Spirit at work in miraculous ways in our lives.

About 75 percent of the people at Northwest Suburban Fellowship had come to faith during the Jesus Movement. We felt at home almost immediately with this group, and it was exciting to be among people who seemed on fire for God. Phil Marsh,[2] the man who started the church, had been a spiritual father to many in the congregation. He had very strong convictions about the way a congregation should be structured so it would function as a first-century church.

It was a familiar claim. Neighborhood Church and each of the Messianic congregations we'd previously attended had also insisted they were in some way like a first-century church. In Phil's case, he believed that the church should be governed by elders, which was a structure familiar to us from our time with the Plymouth Brethren. But Phil believed now that Northwest Suburban Fellowship had moved past its formation phase and was talking about purchasing land and building its own building, his role needed to shift to overseeing the elders, functioning as a modern-day apostle to the congregation. He expected to direct the church from his new position of ultimate authority. The buck would stop with him.

He'd found warrant for his exercise of "apostolic authority" from a group of influential teachers that came to be known as the Fort Lauderdale Five, and also found a theological ally in some of the teachings of the Word of Faith movement. Both of these spiritual viruses first appeared in charismatic circles, but each has con-

---

2. Not his real name.

Chapter 5

tinued to mutate, spreading within evangelicalism in ways none of us could have imagined in the 1980s.

The Century of the Holy Spirit

The Holy Spirit has been at work in the lives of individual believers and the church since Pentecost.[3] But the twentieth century ushered in waves of intense, supernatural activity that touched most every stream of the church, from Orthodox to mainline to evangelical to Catholic. The century opened with a prayer by Pope Leo XIII dedicating the new century to the Holy Spirit just after midnight on January 1, 1901.[4]

But the pope probably couldn't have imagined what followed beginning in 1901 at Bethel Bible College in Topeka, Kansas, when a student named Agnes received the gift of tongues during a prayer meeting.[5] A chain of events unfolded over the next five years as Agnes's experience was duplicated in the lives of others one or two at a

---

3. Acts 2 recounts what it looked like for the community of believers to receive the outpouring of the Holy Spirit, and the rest of the book highlights the variety of ways in which the primitive church experienced his ministry. The ministry of the Holy Spirit included signs and wonders such as courage in the face of persecution (Acts 23), revelation and words of supernatural insight (Acts 10), as well as healings (Acts 14:8-18), deliverance from demonic oppression (Acts 16:16-18), speaking in other tongues (Acts 19:1-7), and other mind-bending miracles (Acts 19:11-12). The Holy Spirit, given through the Son, exists to glorify the Father and empower believers to live lives that reflect God's love and holiness. What follows are a few key New Testament passages regarding the Holy Spirit: regarding the promise and purpose of the Holy Spirit— John 1:29-34; 14:15-31; 20:21-23; Acts 1:8; regarding the gifts (charisms) of the Holy Spirit in the life of the believer: Rom. 12:3-8; 1 Cor. 12-14; 2 Tim. 1:6-7.

4. Julia Duin, "Pentecostalism from Soup to Nuts: A (Near) Complete History of This Movement in America," Get Religion, February 2, 2023, https://tinyurl.com/3f738eb9.

5. "The New Face of Global Christianity: The Emergence of 'Progressive Pentecostalism,'" Pew Research Center, April 12, 2006, https://tinyurl.com/6ryh842t.

Grief Is a Part of the Process

time, until revival exploded in a rented African Methodist Episcopal Church on Azusa Street in Los Angeles. People thronged to the site for the next three years to receive the baptism of the Holy Spirit as evidenced by speaking in unknown tongues. From there, the Pentecostal fire spread to a variety of cities and towns.[6] Azusa Street began as an interracial renewal, but it didn't take long before social forces divided the renewal down the color line, sorting adherents into Black Pentecostal churches and White Pentecostal churches.[7] As Pentecostalism multiplied during the first half of the twentieth century, mainstream evangelicals and mainline denominations tended to keep their tongues-speaking siblings at arm's length.

That changed in April 1960 when the second wave of charismatic renewal began to wash across some mainline churches. Episcopal rector Dennis Bennett told his congregation in Van Nuys, California, that he'd experienced the baptism of the Holy Spirit.[8] Not everyone at his Van Nuys congregation was enthusiastic about this new direction. His denomination transferred him to a dying congregation outside Seattle. The Seattle church exploded in both size and spiritual passion as tongues, deliverance from demonic oppression, prophetic utterance, and healings marked the gatherings. Second-wave charismatics added an interesting theological twist to first-wave Pentecostalism. Professor Nathan Womack explained the differences between the two: "Pentecostals believe that a person must speak in tongues in order to demonstrate that they have been baptized in the Spirit. Charismatics claim that although many people do speak in tongues as their first sign, it is not the only sign that accompanies being baptized in the Holy Spirit. Any manifestations of the gifts of the Holy Spirit outlined

6. Vinson Synan, "Pentecostalism: William Seymour," Christian History Institute, accessed September 27, 2024, https://tinyurl.com/22rb9ucc.

7. David D. Daniels, "Why Pentecostalism's Multiethnic Beginning Floundered," *Christianity Today*, accessed September 27, 2024, https://tinyurl.com/2a2cj3xw.

8. Dennis Bennett, "God's Strength for This Generation," HealMyLife.com, accessed September 27, 2024, https://tinyurl.com/47bnmhdx.

Chapter 5

in the New Testament are recognized by Charismatics as being baptized in the Spirit."[9]

But that wasn't the only twist. For the first half of the twentieth century, to identify as a Pentecostal usually meant you were no longer welcome in evangelical or mainline churches. And many Pentecostals scorned the "liberal" theology of the mainline churches and the "dry" worship of fundamentalist and evangelical believers. The second wave blurred those lines of division.

The lines blurred further when the Jesus Movement broke out in the late 1960s. The site of much of the original activity of the Jesus Movement was Calvary Chapel in Costa Mesa, California. Its pastor, Chuck Smith, had been ordained through a Pentecostal denomination, the International Church of the Foursquare Gospel. Other key figures in the movement's early days, including evangelists Arthur Blessitt and Lonnie Frisbee, also came from Pentecostal backgrounds. First-wave Pentecostalism took on the character of second-wave charismatic expression when it merged with the hippie culture of the Jesus Movement. (There would be one more wave to come a few years later that emerged from this fusion. We'll explore the third-wave Charismatic movement in more detail in the next chapter.)

At the Crossroads

Northwest Suburban Fellowship had been fertilized by two toxic teachings that sprang up at the crossroads of first-wave Pentecostalism and second-wave charismatic renewal: Word of Faith and Shepherding.

Word of Faith. This teaching emerged in the middle of the twentieth century through the ministry of Baptist preacher E. W. Ken-

---

9. Nathan Womack, "Charismatic Renewal Movement in Christianity: Second Wave Pentecostalism," University of British Columbia, August 10, 2020, https://tinyurl.com/3acmp4p6.

Grief Is a Part of the Process

yon, though its roots go back to the rise of New Thought and Christian Science a century earlier.[10] The essential message of Word of Faith teaching is that a confession of faith in prayer unlocks God's storehouses of blessing that rightfully belong to believers because of the finished work of Christ. Also known as positive confession, the prosperity gospel, or, colloquially, "name it and claim it," variations of this notion took hold among some popular midcentury non-Pentecostal American preachers like Robert Schuller and Norman Vincent Peale. It found a home during the same time period in the Pentecostal world first through preacher Kenneth Hagin and then among many other popular teachers that followed, including Kenneth Copeland, Benny Hinn, Creflo Dollar, Paula White, Joyce Meyer, and T. D. Jakes.[11]

Bill and I first encountered Word of Faith at Northwest Suburban Fellowship through conversations with other members, like the woman in our small group who threw away her prescription eyeglasses because she'd claimed God's healing for her myopia. (She showed up a few weeks later wearing glasses again because she hadn't yet received the healing she'd claimed in prayer but told us she was still believing God for it.) We heard it in the ways people talked about illness or financial trials: only a lack of faith was blocking our ability to receive that healing or monetary blessing we'd claimed.

I remember reviewing a Sunday school curriculum church leaders were contemplating using. It was created by Word of Faith children's minister Willie George, popularly known as "Gospel Bill." One of the first lessons in the material taught children how to pray in faith, using the example of a little boy who wanted a

---

10. For more about the roots of New Thought and Christian Science, see "What Is the New Thought Movement?," Got Questions, accessed October 2, 2024, https://tinyurl.com/pw4khvx8.

11. Dmitry Rozet, "The Word of Faith Movement and Positive Confession," SATS, October 23, 2020, https://tinyurl.com/yc5fpdh3; Jack Zavada, "Word of Faith Movement History," Learn Religions, updated December 10, 2018, https://tinyurl.com/3pbvf2ds.

Chapter 5

new skateboard. Because the boy believed without doubt that the angels would bring him a new skateboard, he got his miracle. I raised a red flag but was told by church leaders that there just weren't any good mainstream children's church curriculums that could help children grow spiritually like this material did. At the time, I assumed my questions signified that I lacked even a mustard seed's bit of faith. I swallowed my doubts, but when it was my turn to teach, I glossed over the troubling parts of the lessons.

Shepherding. The other significant influence on the life of this young church was the Shepherding movement. The Shepherding movement, also known as the Discipleship movement, emerged out of a meeting between Bob Mumford, Derek Prince, Charles Simpson, and Don Basham, in Fort Lauderdale, Florida, in 1970. By 1974, Ern Baxter had joined them. The Fort Lauderdale Five were concerned about the lack of discipleship and maturity in the church. These men formed Christian Growth Ministries and called for a pyramidal hierarchy of tight control and authority over groups of young believers, a structure that would resonate with anyone familiar with a multilevel marketing organization like Amway, Mary Kay, or Herbalife.

These five men were at the top of the pyramid. Everyone organized below them had to give complete allegiance (and generous financial support) to undershepherds these men had tasked with providing "spiritual covering" to smaller groups or congregations and individuals.[12] Those with shepherding authority would direct their sheep, and their sheep would serve them and do their bidding in the name of "discipleship." Some shepherds believed they had the authority to direct their flock's choices of marriage partners, jobs, and finances.

Even in more informal shepherding networks, those at the top of the local church pyramid were assigned significant authority

---

12. Scriptures used to support the notion of "spiritual covering" include 1 Cor. 11:2-16, 1 Thess. 5:12-13, and 1 Pet. 5:5.

Grief Is a Part of the Process

and control over the lives of those in their care. The emphasis of the leaders in churches like Northwest Suburban was on endlessly refining and purifying the local church—and insisting that the sheep never, ever question their shepherd.[13]

As I would soon find out, it was a recipe for spiritual abuse.

What was happening within Northwest Suburban Fellowship's leadership by the time we arrived at the church in 1986 was a microcosm of what had been unfolding in the Shepherding movement as a whole. By that point, many Pentecostal and Charismatic leaders of the day, including Episcopal priest Dennis Bennett, broadcaster Pat Robertson, and even Word of Faith preacher Kenneth Copeland, had denounced Shepherding teachings as cultish and unscriptural.[14] Eventually, most of the Fort Lauderdale Five would recant their authoritarian, errant teaching, but the damage was done.

At Northwest, the elder team asked founder Phil Marsh to step down, hoping this move would smooth the friction his authoritarian leadership was creating. They never examined the influence his teaching had on them or how it had shaped and deformed the culture of the church. The problems went far deeper than Phil Marsh. Bill and I trusted the elders, who insisted they wanted nothing but the best for us, their cherished sheep.

But as time went on, I found myself stumbling across red flags: the self-congratulatory chatter from the pulpit by the elders that our church was far more spiritual than the other churches in the area, the inward focus of the group, and the sudden disappearance of a few previously committed members. If we asked other church

---

13. Some helpful retrospectives on the Shepherding movement can be found at Jacob Young, "The Shepherding Movement: A Summary," *Medium*, November 30, 2019, https://tinyurl.com/2wuue7jm; Steven Lambert, "Chapter 2: The Discipleship/Shepherding Movement," Charismatic Captivation, accessed October 2, 2024, https://tinyurl.com/y4eem683; "Shepherding Movement: An Idea Whose Time Has Gone?," *Christianity Today*, accessed October 2, 2024, https://tinyurl.com/48rhb2kz.

14. Lambert, "Chapter Two."

Chapter 5

members, "What happened to ___?," they shifted to a new topic as quickly as possible. One Sunday morning, the elders stopped the service after a woman with a recognized prophetic gifting spoke a word of caution to the congregation that not everyone present was living faithfully. It was a stark contrast to the usually innocuous words of encouragement that were called prophetic utterances in the congregation. A couple of elders escorted her out the back doors of the sanctuary, and the other elders told the worship team to keep playing music as if nothing had happened.

By this point, we'd been active, involved members of the church for six years. Bill and I sensed something was brewing under the surface. I'd previously written a few skits for occasional special services for the congregation, and the lead elder, Dave, approached me about writing a contemporary Good Friday play. I created a draft of a piece that featured a pastor with a heart that had grown cold but had experienced an awakening when he was confronted with someone in need. I tried to communicate in the script that repentance is the gift that Jesus offers each one of us, no matter what our role in the church. My growing concerns about what was happening among the leaders of Northwest Suburban Fellowship may have inspired the plot, but the play's message of hope and renewal was my prayer for the church.

I was invited to do a read-through of the script with the elder, his assistant, and their wives. We were partway through the draft when Dave exploded. He spent most of the next hour screaming at me, questioning my motives, my faith, and my loyalty to the church. The other three sat in silence. Blindsided by his rage, so did I.

When I left that meeting, I felt like I'd been beaten up and robbed. What followed over the next few months compounded the moral injury I'd experienced, as Dave and the rest of the elders launched a vicious gossip campaign against me. My husband and I sought to try to clear the air over the next year, but the leadership team told us on more than one occasion that Dave "had a short fuse" and it was my fault that he lost his temper. When staying became untenable, we met with them to finalize our departure. The

Grief Is a Part of the Process

elder team then expressed their full support of Dave and washed their hands of my family after our years in the congregation. We experienced shunning from most of those with whom we'd worshiped at Northwest Suburban Fellowship. The abysmal behavior from the elder team confirmed my suspicions: there was something rotten at the heart of the congregation. My ability to trust the leadership of a church would never be the same.

It took another decade before the truth came out: Dave had for years dealt with a porn addiction and had been involved in an inappropriate relationship with a congregant. This finally came to light when Dave's wife decided to divorce him. The other elders had known about all of this for a very long time, and had covered for him, choosing instead to demonize anyone who had gotten too close to the truth. They didn't want to do anything to jeopardize the fast-growing church after they'd been through the drama of forcing founder Phil Marsh to step down. Instead they circled their wagons around one of their own in the name of their own spiritual authority, all while insisting they could manage Dave's sin—and their own.

Going Viral in Evangelicalism

The Pentecostal and Charismatic movements of the twentieth century gave some parts of the church a taste of what the book of Acts might have looked like. God was at work today! Those movements energized and renewed the faith of many. They also tapped into a desire for supernatural spiritual power—a desire that flourished in the soil of misplaced emphasis.

The message that God wanted to bless his faithful ones with happiness, health, wealth, and skateboards blended seamlessly with the Pentecostal quest for supernatural power. While the more outrageous claims of televangelists and Word of Faith teachers stayed within that segment of Pentecostalism, the prosperity message seeped into mainstream evangelicalism in subtle ways by suggesting that if the faithful followed prescribed formulas extracted from Scripture,

Chapter 5

they'd unlock God's blessing in their lives. This promise showed itself in popular evangelical subculture in all kinds of ways including finances (Larry Burkett's Christian Financial Concepts curriculum, which was followed by the rise of broadcaster Dave Ramsey's Financial Peace University, both of which were used by thousands of churches), relationships (the Christian parenting advice doled out by influential radio host and author Dr. James Dobson), and a guaranteed happy ever after (the messaging that young people save their virginity for marriage with the True Love Waits campaign).

And there was plenty of ground support for these messages in local congregations. These messages were amplified with sermon series like "Seven Steps to a Successful Marriage" or youth retreats focused on sexual purity. The prosperity gospel in broader evangelical culture subtly shifted the focus from seeking God to procuring his blessings. Those formulas turned faith into a transaction that promised a Christian-ish version of the American Dream.

Likewise, the teachings about authority emerging from the Shepherding movement spread far beyond Pentecostal and Charismatic circles. Of course, the desire for control is nothing new. The Fort Lauderdale Five baptized the lust for power in a pyramid-scheme arrangement for their charismatic audience. However, they weren't the only influential teachers speaking to the evangelical world about authority in the wake of the Jesus Movement. Many new believers in that era had come to faith carrying with them a history of family dysfunction. They were longing for the care of a spiritual parental figure to guide them. In 1961, Bill Gothard launched his Campus Teams ministry with his surefire "biblical" formula for successful living. Through his ministry, rebranded in 1974 as the Institute of Basic Life Conflicts, then again in 1989 as the Institute in Basic Youth Conflicts, Gothard spread his authority-heavy, rule-focused version of the successful Christian life. By 1980, over two million people had attended his weeklong seminars.[15]

15. "The Gothard Files: The Early Years, 1965–79," Recovering Grace, February 11, 2024, https://tinyurl.com/bdd8xk2h.

Grief Is a Part of the Process

His famous "Umbrella of Authority" illustration captured his iron-clad belief in submission, authority, and a "biblical" chain of command. His formula worked in much the same way as a set of Russian nesting dolls. Christ is our huge umbrella sheltering all, and directly underneath him, a smaller umbrella represented a pastor's role, providing spiritual covering to all those in his care. Beneath the pastor, a still smaller umbrella, which represented the husband's role as protector and provider for his family. The wife was pictured as a smaller umbrella, directly under her husband, and her small umbrella, tucked underneath all the progressively larger umbrellas sheltering her, was just large enough for her to exercise her authority in the areas of childbearing and home management. The message was clear: if you stayed under your umbrella of authority, you'd be safe from all of life's storms. (We'll be looking further at Gothard's influence in chapter 7.)

Evangelicalism has long been a hospitable environment for authoritarian personalities preaching big ideas and drawing big crowds. One vivid example is Mark Driscoll. Beginning in the late 1990s, he had a meteoric rise to a national (and international) spotlight as a speaker, author, leader of Seattle-based multisite congregation Mars Hill Church; developer of the Acts 29 network of associated churches; and one of the cofounders of the Gospel Coalition theological organization. His dynamic, unfiltered public persona drew crowds, while his authoritarian leadership style crushed those in his orbit. By 2014, he was no longer in any of these roles, due almost entirely to his history of abusing his power. He lay low for a time, never repenting, then, despite the negative publicity around him, he launched a new church in Arizona. He could still draw a crowd.

Driscoll was far from an isolated example. Too many "talented" communicators caught in moral failure would disappear for a while in what was the adult equivalent of a toddler time-out, then step into the spotlight again somewhere new. Too many evangelicals were willing to misapply Jesus's forgiveness to these leaders, whitewashing the leader's sin. Too few were willing to

Chapter 5

talk about character, consequences, or what Scripture had to say about disqualifying a person from leadership. Too few were willing to take a long look at the trail of wounded sheep these noxious leaders left in their wake.

Downsizing: Grief Is a Part of the Process

Downsizing is a challenging process when you've willingly chosen it. It is another thing entirely when it has been pressed into your life by circumstances beyond your control. If you've ever walked through the valley of the shadow in the wake of an unexpected death of a loved one, or gone through a divorce you didn't want, you have found yourself immersed in the experience of uninvited downsizing. The grief of loss and unwelcome change is embedded in the downsizing process. And spiritual downsizing often carries a high relational cost.

This kind of downsizing will reveal that some people you once counted as friends were not true friends, after all. People you thought you could trust turned out to be betrayers. People who promised to be your spiritual family abused or abandoned you. In the wake of these kinds of traumatic losses, disorienting grief remains. That grief never disappears entirely, though we may over time integrate it into our lives as we move into the future.

That process can also clarify what is of lasting value, and what needs to be torched. Some things don't even deserve the dignity of a trip to the trash heap. I'll be frank: the many variations of Word of Faith and Shepherding teachings need to go directly to the burn pile. They distort Scripture's truths for their own selfish ends. But before we light the match, we need to engage in a treasure hunt guided by the painful question: What drew so many of us— including me—to authoritarian leaders and toxic teachings?

Authoritarian churches are a lure to those longing to receive the sheltering care of a protective parent. The prosperity message is fueled by our core yearning for security. Those are good and

Grief Is a Part of the Process

holy desires that have been used as weapons of coercion in the hands of abusive leaders. True pastors honor the desire for protection and security that God has hardwired within each of us. They recognize that no matter what our age, we are all "little ones" who deserve loving care and life-giving guidance that help us follow our Good Shepherd.

Jesus used very strong language to advocate for vulnerable people: "If anyone causes one of these little ones—those who believe in me—to stumble, it would be better for them to have a large millstone hung around their neck and to be drowned in the depths of the sea" (Matt. 18:6). A culture of control and warped teaching has left immeasurable spiritual damage in the lives of trusting believers.

For those with eyes to see, that damage is where the church's true treasure lies, though a lot of it is buried under the wreckage of religious trauma. One network of therapists describes religious trauma as emerging from faith experience that is "stressful, degrading, dangerous, abusive, or damaging. Traumatic religious experiences may harm or threaten to harm someone's physical, emotional, mental, sexual, or spiritual health and safety."[16] The work of downsizing includes seeking the treasure of those who've been traumatized by bad leaders and toxic teaching. This is the exact opposite inclination of those focused on pursuing power and wealth via spiritual means. Even if evangelicals are willing to root out and dispose of the effects of Shepherding and Word of Faith teaching, that purge won't have done its downsizing work in the church until we are also committed to pursuing grieving and hurting sheep the way Jesus does.

The appendix at the end of this book has a listing of resources for those who've experienced spiritual abuse, and for all of us to become trauma-informed. Because as I discovered as I continued

---

16. Brooks Baer, "Religious Trauma: Signs, Symptoms, Causes, and Treatment," Therapist, May 16, 2024, https://tinyurl.com/5tkv5h3r.

Chapter 5

to seek a faith community after my experience of spiritual abuse, wolves dressed in shepherd's clothing exist in many different streams of evangelicalism.

Reflect

1. In what ways (if any) have you seen the prosperity gospel at work in the congregation(s) in which you've been a part? What messages did your church pass on to you about trials, losses, and suffering?
2. Who is considered a spiritual authority in the church or churches where you've worshiped? What qualifies them to be in that role? Have you experienced the care of a good shepherd? What effect did that have in your life? Conversely, have you witnessed or experienced a leader abusing his power? How did this affect you?
3. Is the notion of religious trauma familiar to you? What might it look like if a church was trauma-informed?

6

Chaos versus Clarity

After our family left Northwest Suburban Fellowship, Bill and I were too battered to look for another church right away. In the early 1990s, there weren't any voices in the circles in which we'd traveled who recommended that sufferers of spiritual abuse consider taking a break from church or get counseling from a professional experienced in dealing with religious trauma, so we soldiered on.

We tried home churching with a couple of other families who'd left Northwest Suburban around the same time we did. There were eight kids aged nine and under, plus seven adults in our little *ecclesia*. Most of our Friday night home-church gatherings were spent trying to keep the kids entertained or breaking up their squabbles. After a few months, we were all exhausted by the effort and ended our experiment.

Bill and I decided we'd try an institutional church that offered children's programming. A couple of friends who knew what we'd been through suggested a nearby Vineyard congregation. The Vineyard movement was charismatic, but from the very first notes of the very first song at the very first worship service we attended,

Chapter 6

I realized this was an entirely different kind of charismatic expression than we'd experienced at Northwest Suburban.

To begin with, the worship music was unfamiliar to me. Almost all of it was written by Vineyard worship leaders, and the vibe was California mellow folk-rock, with songs like "Refiner's Fire" and "Change My Heart, O God" that eventually became standards in many evangelical churches. This difference in music wasn't entirely unexpected, because one of the founders of the Vineyard movement, John Wimber, had been involved in the music business before he came to faith in Christ in the 1960s. He'd then been a part of Chuck Smith's Calvary Chapel, where a lot of Jesus music first originated. By the late 1970s, Wimber, Kenn Gulliksen, and Smith's protégé, evangelist Lonnie Frisbee, had parted ways with Calvary Chapel and planted the first Vineyard congregation in Los Angeles.[1] The Vineyard model multiplied rapidly, and musicians in their churches enjoyed great openness to create new music that flowed out of what people were experiencing during services.

We learned that the high point of Vineyard services came after the sermon, as the "official" part of the service wound down. It was called ministry time, when the pastor would pray over the congregation, sometimes offering a gentle word of knowledge ("Is there someone here who has been dealing with a back problem?") before inviting anyone in need to the front of the sanctuary (in a rented high school theater space) for prayer ministry with members of the congregation's prayer team.

I'd always imagined that people going forward for prayer at the end of a service were seeking salvation, like I'd seen on Billy Graham TV specials or during visits to Baptist churches. But at the Vineyard, the prayer teams were for believers. There was a palpable sense that God would respond to the cries of his hurting children.

---

1. "What Is the Vineyard? Our History," Vineyard USA, March 25, 2016, https://tinyurl.com/mu36bey5.

Chaos versus Clarity

While my unaddressed religious trauma left me in a state of constant vigilance, I did begin to relax a bit in the church as time went on. Our kids seemed to settle into their Sunday school classes. It was a relief to have some structure after our home-church experiment. At the time, I assumed this is what healing must feel like. But after a year or so at the church, the fragile scabs were ripped off my wounds.

One Sunday morning early in 1994, a small group returned from an investigatory visit to the Toronto Airport Christian Fellowship. Word had spread through the Vineyard grapevine that some sort of revival had broken out up there. That small group brought back a souvenir of their visit: a phenomenon that came to be called "holy laughter"—seemingly uncontrollable, prolonged bouts of intense laughter. We were told this was an expression of God's joy, and it was meant to bring healing to hurting souls. This eerie, explosive laughter erupted without warning during worship, in the middle of sermons, and during weekly communion, spreading here and there to pockets of willing people across the congregation. The outpouring of the Holy Spirit in Acts 2 was accompanied by the sound of rushing wind, the sight of flames of fire, and the preaching of the gospel that created upheaval to the regularly scheduled program. We were told that the uncontrollable shaking, laughter, groaning, heavenly visions, roaring and other animal sounds, and weeping during church services was just like Acts 2: a mark of revival.

I longed for the pastor to bring some sort of order to the bedlam. But he told the congregation he never wanted to be the one who quenched the Holy Spirit's work among us. I understood his caution but was frustrated that none of the church leaders seemed to question whether this uncontrolled laughter was of God or ask what its lasting purpose might be. During ministry time at the end of the service, people were falling in slow motion to the ground in ecstasy and surrender, an experience first-wave Pentecostals called being slain in the Spirit, often combined with uncontrollable

Chapter 6

laughter. The church began drawing a whole lot of curious charismatics from other churches in search of the next big thing.

After weeks of this, I told my husband I could not bear going to those wild Sunday morning services any longer. He agreed. No one ever sought us out to find out why we stopped attending. They were too busy chasing revival to pursue wounded sheep like us.

Revive Us Again and Again

The hunger for revival was not limited to the young Vineyard movement. It has always been core to evangelical identity. Historian David Bebbington noted, "Revivalism is a form of activism, involvement in a movement producing conversions not in ones and twos but *en masse*."[2] Just as conversionism frequently is connected to a crisis-based decision to follow Jesus, revivalism is a crisis experience that moves believers whose spiritual life may have grown cold toward a reignited faith.

However, revival means different things to different evangelical constituencies:

- A weeklong series of nightly evangelistic meetings led by a visiting preacher.
- A spontaneous wave of repentance that sweeps through a worship service, culminating in an emotional, tearful rush to the altar so congregants can publicly confess their sin.
- Personal spiritual renewal that results in an increased commitment to practice the classic Christian disciplines such as prayer, service, witness, and Bible reading/study.
- A widespread phenomenon that brings all of culture into sudden alignment with traditional Judeo-Christian values.
- Something that is described in the pages of Scripture, such as

2. David Bebbington, "What Is Revivalism?," *Christianity Today*, accessed September 27, 2024, https://tinyurl.com/mr2bdu34.

Chaos versus Clarity

in the accounts of Ezra and Nehemiah, when an entire nation turns to God.

· The witness of a vibrant local church.

My definition of revival is spiritual renewal initiated by God resulting in conviction of personal and corporate sin, a desire for holiness, and a reordering of both individual life and church community to reflect God's reign. I do believe revival can be contagious, influencing the surrounding culture for good, though not in the viral form we witnessed during the Toronto Blessing days.

Though the hope of revival has shaped evangelicalism, it seems that true revival's manufactured mirror image, revivalism, was the real driver in many church and denominational settings. If you squint, revival and revivalism might look nearly identical. However, revivalism tends to work toward the goal of revival via a programmed, often emotionally manipulative approach—for example, preaching a fiery sermon intended to guide people toward the crisis of experiencing deep shame over their own sinfulness, followed by a series of altar calls that allows them to find relief and resolution of that distress.

That isn't to say that true revival will not release a deeply emotional response: Nehemiah 8:9 tells us that the people of Judah were weeping as they heard the words of the law being read to them and realized how far they'd drifted from God. Revivalism manipulates people toward the goal of "revival." Scripture never prescribes revivalism—but it is the experience with which most of us are familiar.

We have a long history of both revival and revivalism in this country, and they often happen simultaneously.[3] Theologian Scot McKnight observed that revivalism in the middle of the twentieth century was captured in mainstream evangelicalism in things like

3. Patrick Morley, "A Brief History of Spiritual Revival and Awakening in America," *Church Leaders*, October 12, 2022, https://tinyurl.com/2z72addr.

Chapter 6

Billy Graham's preaching, the popularity of the expository Bible teaching of Henrietta Mears, and pastor D. James Kennedy's Evangelism Explosion. McKnight notes, "[Revivalism uses] manufactured, institutionalized, and predictable evangelism techniques ... [for] working harder at decisions than disciples; it's pointing a long finger at a thin soteriology without a robust theology, Christology, pneumatology and ecclesiology."[4]

But those manufactured efforts in mainstream evangelicalism were nothing compared to the hunger for revival—and the temptation to settle for revivalism—that have long existed in Pentecostal and charismatic circles. The last chapter highlighted the first and second waves of Pentecostal/Charismatic renewal in the early and middle years of the twentieth century. But a third wave was birthed in evangelical circles beginning in the late 1970s. Some mark the beginning of this neocharismatic movement to a class taught by C. Peter Wagner and John Wimber at California's evangelical bastion, Fuller Theological Seminary. The class, MC510: Signs, Wonders, and Church Growth, was part lecture and part laboratory where students would ask the Holy Spirit to move among them, and miracles, tongues, and deliverances followed, sparking both renewal and controversy on campus.[5] The class was canceled eventually, but it fueled the launch of a new kind of church, the Vineyard. With it, a new wave of charismatic expression was born.

This third wave merged evangelical sensibilities with what some in the movement called "the power gifts" of healing, prophetic insight, and deliverance. John Wimber challenged his evangelical siblings in faith to show and tell the whole gospel, confirmed with signs and wonders: "He called us as kingdom people, doing the stuff of proclamation and demonstration. To do only half

---

4. Scot McKnight, "Revivalism: What Is It?," *Scot's Newsletter*, March 3, 2022, https://tinyurl.com/3hfk2d6m.

5. "Disruption: Past and Future," Fuller Studio, accessed September 27, 2024, https://tinyurl.com/awset8z4.

Chaos versus Clarity

of what we've been called into is not a complete Gospel message and we must do all of what God's placed upon us."[6]

Some freshly empowered evangelicals stayed in their original churches, but many moved into Vineyard or Vineyard-adjacent congregations. Former evangelical cessationists like theology professors Sam Storms and Jack Deere sought to bridge the gap between mainstream evangelicals and their third-wave siblings.[7]

But the third wave didn't happen ex nihilo. A couple of fringe teachings that had bubbled up in first-wave Pentecostal circles after the end of World War II fueled the thinking of some influential third-wave leaders: the Latter Rain Revival and the Healing Revival. Latter Rain focused on the restoration of the gifts to the church in the last days, which Latter Rain proponents dated to the founding of the State of Israel in May 1948 as a Jewish homeland. The revival drew its name from the prophecy of Joel 2:28; adherents believed the "latter rains" were to be a last-days outpouring of the Holy Spirit that would be even greater than the first outpouring at Pentecost. Linked with this was the Healing Revival, which focused on displays of physical restoration. Oral Roberts and William Branham were key names in the healing movement.[8] The Latter Rain and Healing Revivals often overlapped

6. "Quotes from John Wimber," Vineyard USA, accessed September 27, 2024, https://tinyurl.com/ytj6rt8u.

7. Pastor and author Sam Storms parsed some of the core theology of the Holy Spirit that emerged from this third wave: "Most Third Wave believers do not believe that the baptism in the Holy Spirit is a distinct experience separate from conversion . . . [they] do not insist that speaking in tongues is the initial physical evidence of baptism in the Spirit. Many will receive the gift of tongues at the time of their conversion, but most will experience this manifestation of the Spirit at some time subsequent to their being born again. And unlike their Pentecostal cousins, those in the Third Wave do not believe that God intends for every Christian to receive this particular gift." Sam Storms, "Pentecostals, Charismatics, and the Third Wave: Who Believes What? Part Two," Sam Storms, May 5, 2021, https://tinyurl.com/y5sm9595.

8. Oral Roberts went on to more mainstream acceptance in the Pen-

Chapter 6

and initially sought to bring renewal to Pentecostalism. Many established Pentecostal groups resisted these novel emphases and fringe theology.[9]

There was an alarming pattern of moral failure and the preaching of increasingly unorthodox doctrine in the mid-twentieth century among some key Latter Rain and Healing Revival leaders.[10] Latter Rain and Healing teachings never became fully mainstream but served as an outsized influence on some of what unfolded in the decades to come, specifically in what came to be known in the first decades of the twenty-first century as New Apostolic Reformation. (We'll be exploring that topic further in chapter 9.)

However, in 1994, revival was the primary focus of many third-wave charismatics. John and Carol Arnott, pastors of the Toronto Airport Vineyard, traveled to South America to witness the ministry of evangelist Claudio Freidzon. They received what they

---

tecostal world, becoming a well-known televangelist and founder of his namesake university in Tulsa, Oklahoma. William Branham drifted into serious theological error that put him far outside the bounds of orthodoxy: Dave Littlewood, "William Branham—the Prophet of Controversy," New Life Publishing, February 5, 2022, https://tinyurl.com/2kvn6zzh.

9. Latter Rain leaders taught that God was restoring the "fivefold ministry" (leadership gifts named in Ephesians 4:11, which include apostle, evangelist, prophet, teacher, pastor) of the Holy Spirit to the church: the baptism of the Holy Spirit as evidenced with tongues could be received through the "laying on of hands" of another person in prayer; denominations would cease to exist and the church would organize, as in the first century, via geographical region; and some believers would receive incorruptible spiritual bodies here on this earth that would allow them to be translated instantaneously from one location to another in order to preach the gospel. "Latter Rain Movement," Theopedia, accessed October 2, 2024, https://tinyurl.com/2s97pzn4.

10. A sampling: "Latter Rain Movement," Theopedia; "What Is the Latter Rain Movement?," Got Questions, accessed October 2, 2024, https://tinyurl.com/d75rpswy; Littlewood, "William Branham"; Andrew Strom, "Great Healing Revivalists—How God's Power Came," accessed October 2, 2024, https://tinyurl.com/22pup6bc.

Chaos versus Clarity

believed was a greater anointing from God for ministry during that visit. After that, they invited St. Louis Vineyard pastor Randy Clark to speak at their church, as he was similarly God-hungry. Arnott described what followed:

> We had been praying for God to move, and had assumed that we would see people saved and healed, but when ministry time came, everything exploded. God's power and anointing were ramped up from anything we'd ever seen. We weren't doing anything different, but the Father's blessing fell on the 120 people attending that Thursday night meeting, January 20, 1994. It hadn't occurred to us that God would throw a massive party where people would laugh, roll, cry and become so empowered that emotional hurts from childhood would just lift off. Some people were so overcome physically by God's power they had to be carried out.[11]

The "Toronto Blessing" was not embraced by all Charismatic evangelicals. The church in Toronto chose to disaffiliate from the Vineyard in 1996 over Vineyard leaders' concerns about charismatic excesses there and the way the renewal was being stewarded by the Arnotts and other leaders.[12] Wimber addressed the parting of the ways: "Our decision was to withdraw endorsement; their decision was to resign."[13] Not long after this, Metro Vineyard Fellowship, pastored by Mike Bickle in Kansas City, disaffiliated for similar reasons.[14]

11. John Arnott and Carol Arnott, "The Toronto Blessing: What Is It?," *John and Carol* (blog), December 31, 1999, https://tinyurl.com/5aw96m8d.

12. The church changed its name to Toronto Airport Christian Fellowship in 1996, then rebranded again in 2010 to Catch the Fire Toronto.

13. Tim Stafford and Jim Beverley, "God's Wonder Worker," *Christianity Today*, July 14, 1997, https://tinyurl.com/yc57fdd3.

14. James A. Beverley, "Leading Church Leaves Association," *Christianity Today*, October 7, 1996, https://tinyurl.com/3x4jca8e.

Chapter 6

There were similar large-scale outbreaks of holy laughter elsewhere during the 1990s, including in Colombia, in the United Kingdom through the New Frontiers International network of churches and in the Anglican church Holy Trinity Brompton, and in the Brownsville Assembly of God in Pensacola, Florida.

During the 1990s, the Brownsville Assembly of God drew over five thousand people a night for six years, with some estimates suggesting that more than two million people streamed to the church from all over the world during that period. The church added staff and built a giant sanctuary. But when the renewal faded and the crowds moved on, the church found itself $11.5 million in debt.[15]

Some congregations who were influenced by the mix of Toronto Blessing, Latter Rain, and Healing teachings launched new ministries or shifted existing ones in radically different directions. The teaching and music production emerging from three third-wave hubs influenced churches all over the world. By 1999 in Kansas City, Mike Bickle shifted the former Metro Vineyard to become a 24/7 house of prayer. Bethel, a traditional Assemblies of God congregation in Redding, California, became a magnet for those seeking physical healing. Another in New South Wales, Australia, eventually became a worship music powerhouse and international multisite church, Hillsong.

Those three congregations have also courted more than their share of controversy. Facing multiple credible allegations of sexual and spiritual abuse, Bickle separated from his International House of Prayer in December 2023—and as of this writing, the ministry, which has been rocked by a series of other moral scandals, is in the process of "reorganizing."[16] The toxic culture at Hillsong was

15. "Church of Famed 'Brownsville Revival' Struggles," American Press, March 30, 2012, https://tinyurl.com/22y62f26.

16. Judy L. Thomas, "IHOPKC Confirms 'Inappropriate Behavior,' Announces Permanent Split with Founder Bickle," *Kansas City Star*, March 25 2024, https://tinyurl.com/bdkxh8n4; Heidi Schmidt, "International House of Prayer KC Announces Changes, Closure," KCTV5, April 16, 2024, https://tinyurl.com/4h2rrbx6.

Chaos versus Clarity

profiled in the 2022 documentary series *Hillsong: A Megachurch Exposed*. Additionally, Hillsong founder Brian Houston left his position at the church in 2022 after he faced charges that he'd covered up his father's child sexual abuse crimes. His father, Assemblies of God pastor Frank Houston, died before he faced a legal reckoning.[17] And rumors of bizarre practices and heretical teaching have circled around Bethel in Redding for years.[18]

Downsizing: Chaos versus Clarity

When you dive into the nitty-gritty of the physical downsizing process, it will look like chaos at first as closets are emptied and the contents lurking in the dark corners of cabinets see the light of day. Perhaps the corollary to the adage "It's always darkest before the dawn" is "It's always most chaotic before the downsizing begins in earnest."

Revivalism birthed a culture of immaturity in some charismatic circles, where character took a back seat to dramatic displays of spiritual power and emotional goosebumps replaced holiness. People who experienced a mountaintop supernatural experience still had to live out their discipleship journey in the trenches of their daily life, and the disconnect between the two was jarring for many. Some resorted to chasing the next revival-type event. Others faded away in discouragement.

---

17. "Hillsong Church Founder Brian Houston Found Not Guilty of Concealing His Father's Child Sex Crimes," Associated Press, August 17, 2023, https://tinyurl.com/4mvh68r5.

18. A sampling: Carrie Lloyd, "Grave Sucking and Gold Dust: I Spent 10 Years at Bethel. Here's the Truth behind the Wild Rumours," *Premier Christianity*, November 15, 2021, https://tinyurl.com/27v75p4c; Damon Arthur, "Update: Bethel Pastor Johnson Addresses Attempts to Resurrect Child," *Record Searchlight*, December 17, 2019, https://tinyurl.com/2vyae7aa; Nick Campbell, "Why I'm Still Skeptical of Bethel—Part 1, the One Most Won't Like," *Christ Is the Cure*, May 10, 2022, https://tinyurl.com/5jpdmkbe.

Chapter 6

Fireworks dissipate. Candles have the fuel to burn for a long, long time. Revivalism is fireworks. Revival ignites slow-burning candles.

The church was never meant to be a fireworks factory. Nor is it a spiritual amusement park, a spa, or a flea market, each of which is a descriptor of revivalism. A truly revived church brings order out of chaos, and healing out of relational, physical, and spiritual dysfunction. It is a place meant to be a hospital for sinners. Hebrews 13:20–21 is a prayer that has special resonance to the church's calling to be a people of healing: "Now may the God of peace, who through the blood of the eternal covenant brought back from the dead our Lord Jesus, that great Shepherd of the sheep, *equip* you with everything good for doing his will, and may he work in us what is pleasing to him, through Jesus Christ, to whom be glory for ever and ever. Amen."

The word translated "equip" is the Greek word *katartizo* (kat-ar-tid'-zo). This word is also used in Scripture to describe the process of mending or restoring. Pastor Chad Williams notes, "To equip is to participate with God in the spiritual mending, healing and perfecting of a fellow sinner. And this kind of equipping can only take place within the grace-filled, covenant community of a local church. The church is the only hospital in existence staffed by fellow patients. We are healed, in order to be used by God, to help others heal. As we pour out our lives to mend others something remarkable happens: We are mended too."[19]

To put it another way, we are revived.

Revival and revivalism spur rapid numerical growth in the congregations they touch, which can create a church environment that chases the spiritual quick fix to the diminishment of doing the often-slow work of healing in the form of faithful discipleship. It is not unwarranted that evangelical spirituality has been characterized by some critics as being a mile wide and an inch deep.

19. Chad Williams. "A 'Hospital for Sinners'? (Re-thinking 'Equipping' in the Church)," Develop to Deploy, October 18, 2021, https://tinyurl.com/ywj75ttk.

Chaos versus Clarity

Downsizing, by definition, is about churches and ministries contracting in size. A downsized evangelicalism can bring order out of chaos, focusing our mission of participating with Jesus in his ministry of proclaiming good news to the poor, freedom to the captive, restoring sight to the blind, and setting the oppressed free (Luke 4:18–19, referencing Isa. 61:1–2).

God has given each of us a longing for wholeness. Revival-type signs and wonders are a grace and may serve as an initial catalyst to healing. However, maturity comes from what pastor and author Eugene Peterson called "a long obedience in the same direction."[20] That long obedience characterizes the best of what the community of faith has been over the last two thousand years, and long obedience in the same direction will filter the enchantment with revivalism that has captivated so much of modern evangelicalism.

Reflect

1. Was the word "revival" used in the circles in which you've traveled in evangelicalism? If so, what was it supposed to look like? What sorts of things were said to "block" revival from happening? How were Christians encouraged to promote or cultivate revival?

2. Have you witnessed spiritual faddishness or people chasing the next spiritual high or mountaintop moment in the circles in your experience within evangelicalism? How so?

3. What is the relationship between "a long obedience in the same direction" and revivalism?

---

20. Peterson borrowed the phrase from philosopher Frederick Nietzsche for his 1980 book about discipleship, *A Long Obedience in the Same Direction: Discipleship in an Instant Society.*

7

Sort It Out

In 1995, a few months after we last attended the church at the Vineyard, my husband received a job offer in Milwaukee. His daily commute in the Chicago area sometimes took more than two and a half hours, so moving to a smaller city seemed like an opportunity to give our family more quality time together and find a church that would give us (another) fresh start.

By this time, we'd joined the ranks of America's homeschoolers. In the early 1990s, there were an estimated 700,000 homeschoolers in the United States, and the numbers were growing each year.[1] We'd decided to homeschool as an alternative to the underfunded, overcrowded public schools in the northwest suburbs of Chicago. We investigated a couple of small private schools, but the cost was prohibitive for our young family. Bill and I knew a couple of families who'd chosen to homeschool and began a series of investigatory conversations with them in search of answers to

---

1. "Homeschooling in the United States: 1999," National Center for Education Statistics, accessed September 27, 2024, https://tinyurl.com/2whs2685.

questions like "What about socialization?," "Is homeschooling legal?," "How can we find a solid curriculum?," and "Are we crazy for considering this?"

Those friends invited us to attend the Illinois Christian Home Educators state conference to gather more intel. The very first keynote speaker we heard was a pastor named Jonathan Lindvall, who began by explaining that homeschooling was about whole family discipleship. I thought of Deuteronomy 6:4–9, which spoke of parents passing on their faith to the next generation in the natural rhythms of family life. Those words were core to my own Jewish heritage, as well as being a prayer for the kind of home Bill and I hoped to create for our children.

Lindvall's application of those timeless principles was quite extreme. He prescribed "whole family" socialization: no child in his household was ever permitted to have time alone with a peer. If a friend came over to visit, that friend was expected to spend time with the entire Lindvall family. If one of his kids was invited to someone else's home, he insisted the whole family accompany them.[2]

At the time, we dismissed Lindvall as a fringe character with strong opinions who'd been handed a microphone. The rest of the conference was far less weird. It focused on the nuts and bolts of home education with workshops on topics like teaching math, managing record-keeping, and navigating the education laws in our state. That fall, we began homeschooling a kindergartener, first grader, and third grader. Though it wasn't all vinegar and baking soda volcanoes and cozy read-aloud sessions, our kids were learning—and so were we. We continued homeschooling the next year, then the one after that.

2. Lindvall also became known in homeschool circles for his extreme approach to parent-directed betrothal, which resulted in the marriage of his fifteen-year-old daughter to a twenty-eight-year-old man: Kathryn Andes, "Return to Old Premarital Rite: Betrothal," *Fresno Bee*, July 30, 1995, 81, 86, https://tinyurl.com/22yhnp57; Libby Anne, "Child Marriage and the Rest of the Maranatha Story," *Patheos*, December 11, 2013, https://tinyurl.com/4yftzvw3.

Chapter 7

When our family moved to a suburb near the edge of the Milwaukee metropolitan area, we would soon learn that voices like Jonathan Lindvall's weren't as fringe in the homeschool community as we had imagined. After first checking out the public schools in our new town, we elected to continue homeschooling as we began our fourth year of kitchen-table academics.

Bill and I searched for a noncharismatic church that might help us all build new relationships. Though our core convictions about the person and work of the Holy Spirit hadn't changed, we were exhausted by the abuse and emotionalism we'd witnessed in charismatic circles during the previous decade. Through a couple of contacts in the local homeschool community, we found our way to a congregation called Grace Bible Fellowship.[3] Seeing so many homeschooled kids in the congregation on our first visit gave me hope that our kids would find ready friendships in the church—and so would we.

Grace Bible Fellowship was a barebones affair. Many of the sermons from the rotating cast of bivocational preachers tended to be restatements of sermons they'd first heard from the cassette tape "ministries" of their favorite fundamentalist Bible teachers. These teachers emphasized separation from the world. Their source material was supplemented by the growing body of content coming from pastors and leaders associated with the homeschool community, who almost always emphasized the very same thing.

The responsibilities and intense togetherness of homeschooling are like parenting on steroids. Steroids can suppress inflammation, but they come with a host of side effects that include aggression, irritability, blurred vision, and high blood pressure. I discovered what this could look like at one of our first local homeschool support group gatherings. The support group was composed primarily of families from Grace Bible Fellowship, a similar homeschool-centric church in a nearby town, and a brave few from other local evangelical congregations.

3. Grace Bible Fellowship closed its doors in 1998.

Sort It Out

Thursday afternoons were dedicated to homeschool skating at a roller rink. The musical selections for these afternoons came from the canon of children's Sunday school tracks like "Father Abraham Had Many Sons" and "Rise and Shine (The Arky Arky Song)." One afternoon, someone dared to mix in an Amy Grant hit ("Baby, Baby") and a track by the contemporary Christian rock group Petra. Judging by the outrage among a significant portion of the moms that day, you would have thought someone had thrown a couple of Metallica deep cuts into the rotation.

Their musical sins? Petra was using the devil's instruments, electric guitars and drums, and Amy Grant embraced that evil rock beat, then compounded her sin by "crossing over" onto the pop charts.[4] These artists weren't singing the fundamentalist-approved set list of psalms, hymns, and spiritual songs.

The next week at homeschool skate time, about a third of the group didn't show up. There was no way these moms were going to risk exposing their children to Amy Grant's music ever again. The attendance numbers continued to drop in the following weeks, and the rink eventually canceled the event. When this episode was discussed by the homeschool moms at church, most shrugged as if it was no big deal.

The fear-driven overreaction toward even the slightest hint of a perceived cultural threat that seemed to be targeting the family was something we'd experience again and again during our three years in this church community. Uniformity in lifestyle had replaced Christian unity as a value in this small congregation. A church that served only conservative homeschool families looked a lot like the lopsided body Paul warned against in 1 Corinthians 12. In retrospect, it was sadly predictable that the

---

4. Fundamentalist concerns about the "African rhythms," rebellion, and satanic influence in rock music have circulated for decades. Articles like this capture those arguments: Richard Hollerman, "Ten Scriptural Reasons Why the Rock Beat Is Evil in Any Form," True Discipleship, accessed October 2, 2024, https://tinyurl.com/54ajz3zy.

Chapter 7

inward-focused congregation turned on each other. When a theological controversy created a schism in the church, a majority of the members returned as a group to the large congregation from which they'd divided fifteen years earlier. We did not feel led to join them. Within weeks, Grace Bible Fellowship folded, and we were left with another new set of spiritual baggage to add to the mismatched collection we'd been accumulating since the beginning of our marriage.

Our experience spotlighted the reality that the fears that animate us can identify the idols we worship. This idol is so deeply embedded into evangelicalism that it took an intense exposure like we had at Grace Bible Fellowship and the homeschool community in Wisconsin before I could name the claim it had in my life. As I did this, I saw it all around me in evangelicalism, but the place it revealed itself most intensely to me was in the homeschool community.

That idol's name was Family.

Focusing on the Family

Homeschoolers didn't create this idol, of course, But homeschooling subtly amplified the one that had existed in evangelicalism for decades. While Scripture and Christian history upheld the importance of the family as the building block of church and society, the rapid social change that swept through society in the mid-twentieth century heightened the urgency to center the traditional nuclear family in evangelical programming and preaching. Ironically, the modern homeschool movement first grew in the organic soil of 1960s hippie counterculture, cultivated by various collectives of people who moved off the grid into communes so they could reinvent the world. Part of that reinvention included embracing alternative forms of education that included homeschooling.

Home education was nudged toward the Christian mainstream

Sort It Out

by influencers like Dr. James Dobson, whose popular daily radio program, *Focus on the Family*, raised the alarm about the direction and content of public education in America. Dobson was joined by a rising tide of newly minted conservative evangelical political activists who drew their talking points about the secular assault on the traditional family from organizations like Jerry Falwell's Moral Majority. Homeschooling became more than a fringe alternative form of education during these years.[5] It was also becoming a front in the ever-expanding culture war.

The Coalition for Responsible Homeschooling described the shift that took place in home education during the 1980s:

> While early homeschool leaders had focused on liberating children from the constraints of formal schooling and freeing them to follow their interests, these new leaders had a different goal and vision. These new leaders created a radical social and religious vision in which children would be homeschooled with the explicit purpose of being launched into government, education, and the entertainment industries in order to transform the United States into a nation based in Christian beliefs. . . .
> In contrast to the earlier focus on liberating children, these leaders have generally focused on properly training children,

5. First-generation home-educating trailblazers created pathways for other families considering this option through books, kitchen-table-produced magazines like the *Teaching Home* and *Home School Digest*, and state conferences. There were remarkable success stories like the Colfax family, who detailed their experiences in the 1988 book *Homeschooling for Excellence*. At the time they wrote the book, their first three children were Harvard-bound. Mary Pride, a Christian social contrarian with a large family, tackled the how and why of homeschooling in books like *The Way Home: Beyond Feminism, Back to Reality* (1985); *The Big Book of Home Learning* (1986); *The Next Big Book of Home Learning* (1987); and *Schoolproof* (1988). In 1993, she launched her own magazine, *Practical Homeschooling*. I reviewed curriculum for *Practical Homeschooling* for several years during the mid-1990s.

Chapter 7

and in many cases have placed more emphasis on religious ideology than on education.[6]

The messaging we got from many prominent leaders in the homeschool movement was that our kitchen-table multiplication lessons were really about saving our lost culture from itself for the sake of our children. They told us this war was about who would wield power in America and the West, and our weapons in the fight were named Dominionism, Patriarchy, and Purity.

Dominionism

Peter Marshall and David Manuel's 1977 book *The Light and the Glory* offered readers a version of early American history from Columbus's voyage to the Constitution's ratification that recasts it as a uniquely Christian story. Their thesis: "Could it be that we Americans, as a people, had been given a mission by almighty God? . . . And was our vast divergence from this mission, after such a promising beginning, the reason we now seem to be sliding into a morass of moral decay, with our world growing darker by the moment?"[7]

Most history curriculums available to homeschoolers from fundamentalist Christian school publishers like Abeka, Bob Jones University, and A.C.E. School of Tomorrow echoed the same basic ideas, along with an insistence that the US Civil War was a battle over states' rights, not slavery. It has been estimated that at least 75 percent of homeschoolers during the '90s were white.[8] The

6. "A Brief History of Homeschooling," Coalition for Responsible Home-schooling, accessed September 27, 2024, https://tinyurl.com/yfbv4dun.

7. Peter J. Marshall and David Manuel Jr., *The Light and the Glory* (Grand Rapids: Revell, 1977, 2009) 16.

8. "Homeschooling in the United States: 1999," 5.

Sort It Out

steep rise in conservative Christians in this demographic appeared to mean that relatively few were questioning these narratives, nor the kind of theology that was fueling the idea of privileged Christian American greatness.

Dominionism (also known as reconstructionism) is a theology based on the teaching that God ordained Christians to rule their nations according to God's law. Orthodox Presbyterian pastor Rousas J. Rushdoony developed these ideas beginning in the 1960s, and they were embraced by Bible teachers Greg Bahnsen and Gary North, before making their way into the work of a number of others, including lightning-rod pastor and classical educator Douglas Wilson, whose magazine *Credenda Agenda* reached a small but influential audience in the homeschool community beginning in the 1990s.[9]

Dominionists asserted that God had given authority to believing humans, and it was our responsibility to rule according to God's law. Dominionism codified the desires of many homeschoolers who'd withdrawn from the world in search of a culture where "our values" would not only prevail but rule. Diluted forms of dominionism influenced a diverse menu of evangelical leaders far beyond the scope of the homeschool community, including broadcaster Pat Robertson, teacher and cultural critic Francis Schaeffer, and pastors D. James Kennedy and Tim LaHaye.

---

9. Wilson is a vocal proponent for Reformed classical education, and his ministry, based in Moscow, Idaho, has created homeschool curriculums, has launched classical schools and New Saint Andrews College, and engages in debate defending his unapologetic and extreme views on gender roles, theology, and slavery. His ministry has also been on the receiving end of ongoing accusations of spiritual abuse, and has been in legal trouble for his role in enabling and covering up sexual predation within his community: Libby Anne, "Doug Wilson: Jamin Wight Not a 'Sexual Predator,'" *Patheos*, September 22, 2015, https://tinyurl.com/yck6444a.

Chapter 7

Patriarchy

I had a shock of recognition within minutes of watching one of the first episodes of *17 Kids and Counting* on cable network TLC when it premiered in 2008. I knew instantly the Duggars were home-schoolers who were enrolled in Bill Gothard's Advanced Training Institute (ATI) program, because all the kids played stringed instruments, didn't own a TV, and Jim Bob was not just a father but the patriarch of his supersized clan. I'd known carbon copies of the Duggars, right down to the jumper-wearing mothers, in home-schooling circles in Wisconsin.

Gothard had an outsized influence in the homeschool world for decades, even among those of us who didn't subscribe to his curriculum. The never-married Gothard influenced hundreds of thousands of individuals and countless churches with a slate of seminars focused on teaching biblical principles as a formula for success in life, with a heavy emphasis on authority, tradition, and unquestioning obedience.[10]

He took note of the burgeoning homeschool movement in the early 1980s and developed a program for families based on his teaching. ATI offered curriculums covering all subject areas called Wisdom Booklets that were based on his rules-driven interpretation of the Sermon on the Mount. Homeschooling families who wanted to enroll had to first attend his seminars; then fill out an application that included questions about faith, television viewing, commitment to listening only to "harmonious music"; and sign a statement about how many hours a week the father worked.[11] Mothers were expected to be "keepers at home." The success of an ATI family rested on having a strong patriarch guiding the

10. Edward E. Plowman, "Bill Gothard's Institute," *Christianity Today*, May 25, 1973, https://tinyurl.com/yxyurrmr.

11. Advanced Training Institute International, application form, accessed September 27, 2024, https://tinyurl.com/2xe5fvx7.

Sort It Out

family according to the nostalgic ideals and gender roles prismed through Gothard's interpretive lens of the biblical good ol' days, circa 1952.

He was not creating this system in an evangelical vacuum. In the late 1980s, conservative evangelical theologians including Wayne Grudem and John Piper collaborated on the Danvers Statement, a manifesto promoting traditional gender roles as the only biblically faithful response to the rising tide of feminism in both culture and church.[12] In conjunction with this effort, they created the Council for Biblical Manhood and Womanhood, which advocated for complementarianism, a term they coined to explain that men and women have complementary but different roles and responsibilities in the home, at church, and in culture.[13]

Given the intense convictions that draw many to choose homeschooling, it wasn't surprising that complementarianism was a gateway drug to unfiltered, extreme patriarchy for a number of influential homeschool speakers and publications.

During the 1990s, some of the voices advocating for patriarchy included Gothard and Lindvall, whom we'd heard at our first homeschool convention in Illinois, plus Doug Phillips of Vision Forum, Doug Wilson, and authors Michael and Debi Pearl. Magazines including *Patriarch* and *Quit You Like Men* for fathers, and *Gentle Spirit* and *Above Rubies* for mothers, preached the gospel of patriarchy in the homeschool community. Advocacy for patriarchy continued to grow far outside the boundaries of the ever-expanding homeschool world in the following decades, becoming a matter of first-order doctrine among many groups in the fundamentalist wing and some adjacent spaces within evangelicalism.

12. "The Danvers Statement," Council on Biblical Manhood and Womanhood, accessed September 27, 2024, https://tinyurl.com/2d56rys9.

13. During the same period, evangelicals who did not embrace complementarianism created the organization Council for Biblical Equality in order to promote biblically faithful egalitarianism.

Chapter 7

Purity

If it is true that for every action there is an equal and opposite reaction, then the rise of purity culture in the 1980s and 1990s was a predictable reaction to the sexual revolution that was in full flower by that time. The Southern Baptists launched the organization True Love Waits in 1993 to encourage chastity until marriage. Teens were invited to pledge their abstinence. Some families gifted their teens with purity rings they'd wear as a reminder of this commitment through their dating years until they gave it to their spouses on their wedding day.

By 1997, twenty-three-year-old Joshua Harris was the purity standard-bearer, first in the homeschool community, and then crossing over to a wider audience in conservative evangelicalism. Harris was the son of homeschooling pioneers Gregg and Sono Harris. He wrote the best seller *I Kissed Dating Goodbye* to encourage readers to ditch dating entirely for a parent-involved courtship model as the safest, holiest way to find a life partner. After a painful breakup in his teens, Harris wrote, "For the first time I began to question how my faith in Christ affected my love life. There had to more to it than 'don't have sex' or 'date only Christians.' . . . Books like *Passion and Purity* by Elisabeth Elliot and long talks with my dad and mom began to change my perspective."[14] While those of us in the homeschool community had been hearing speakers and writers advocate for a courtship model in our circles, Harris's book moved it toward the mainstream.

Connected to the courtship message among ultraconservative families such as those within Bill Gothard's ATI organization was the call for older teen girls who were finishing their high school years but not yet betrothed to content themselves in the role of "stay-at-home daughters." These young women were told that eschewing college

14. Joshua Harris, *I Kissed Dating Goodbye* (Sisters, OR: Multnomah, 1997), from chapter 1.

Sort It Out

and career and living at home under the authority of their fathers was the only biblical response to feminist messaging in popular culture. Dominionism, patriarchy, and purity messaging intersected in the rationale for single adult women to be "stay-at-home daughters."

Bill and I weren't fans of the dominionist theology or patriarchy, but less-extreme versions of the purity message resonated with us as they seemed a guarantee of happily-ever-after for our children. I ached to protect my children from the hurt and shame I'd experienced due to my own history of promiscuity before I came to faith in Christ. Bill and I encouraged our kids to build healthy friendships with members of the opposite sex, to save their virginity for marriage, and we let them know we were there to partner with them as they sought a spouse when they were ready. As we witnessed our children making their own choices as they stepped into young adulthood, we discovered they heard in our well-intentioned counsel something oppressive due to the amplified version of the purity message ricocheting around the homeschool silo in which we lived during their preteen and early teen years.

The confidence with which so many homeschool speakers spouted their surefire formulas designed to save the family and our society has been unmasked by the domino-like downfall of so many influential homeschooling leaders. Bill Gothard was removed from his ministry in 2014 after a tidal wave of sexual harassment charges spanning decades came to light. Vision Forum's Doug Phillips was removed from ministry in 2013 after reports of sexual abuse of a young woman in his employ became public. Doug Wilson has covered for a man now in prison for pedophilia, been charged with creating a spiritually abusive environment in his church and ministry, and appears to relish creating controversy with his acid takes on social media and in his writing and speaking on topics ranging from slavery to sex.[15]

---

15. Additional reads about these leaders: Suzanne Titkemeyer, "Michael

Chapter 7

Beyond the excruciating saga of the eldest Duggar son's incestuous actions during his teens, the family's cover-up, his online adulterous antics on a dating website, and eventual imprisonment for possession of child porn, there have also been fractured relationships in the once seemingly perfect clan with some of the Duggars' other adult children. And Joshua Harris kissed both his marriage and his Christian faith good-bye in 2019.[16]

A homeschool parent once told me that she used to believe that the instruction she received from the big-name homeschool speakers and writers in the 1990s for creating the godly family of her dreams would allow her to push a spiritual button in her children's lives. By pushing that button she could guide them (or control them) in the way she thought they should go, sparing them—and herself—pain and shame. She realized sadly as her children moved into adulthood that that button had never existed in her children's lives but was wired to the gift she'd allowed to become her idol—her family.

While evangelicalism's focus on the family was especially intense in homeschooling circles, the family has long been an acceptable idol across the broader movement. Many suburban and rural evangelical congregations aim most of their programming

---

and Debi Pearl and That Child Abuse Demonstration," *Patheos*, February 18, 2020, https://tinyurl.com/m2kbkt6p; Shay Seaborne, "The Truth about Cheryl," Shay Seaborne, August 24, 2016, https://tinyurl.com/2zye4nfc; Sarah Stankorb, "That Moscow Mood," *Slate*, December 2, 2023, https://tinyurl.com/4756s5u9.

16. Libby Anne, "A Summary of Allegations against Bill Gothard and IBLP," *Patheos*, January 26, 2016, https://tinyurl.com/yrwswns6; Julie Ingersoll, "Doug Phillips: The Big Scandal You Didn't Hear about and Why It Matters," *Huffington Post*, updated January 23, 2014, https://tinyurl.com/fs f8euwd; Alison Schwartz, Natalie Stone, and People Staff, "A History of the Ups & Downs of the Duggar Family," *People*, updated June 1, 2023, https://tinyurl.com/mh28ptsd; Sarah McCammon, "Evangelical Writer Who Influenced Purity Culture Announces Separation from Wife," NPR, July 21, 2019, https://tinyurl.com/4hanhjph. The Duggar family was also the subject of the 2023 documentary series *Shiny Happy People*.

Sort It Out

toward attracting young families by providing excellent nursery facilities, lively Sunday morning children's programming, vacation Bible school weeks, youth groups, moms groups, marriage enrichment weekends, parenting seminars, family camps, and more. We have "safe for the whole family" Christian entertainment and media options. Focusing on our nuclear family is an expression of our individualized understanding of our faith.

The last decade has seen a steep rise in local evangelical political action animated by culture-war fears surrounding family issues, including which books are available on public library shelves and what is in the curriculum being taught in public school classrooms. Despite all this energy expended to protecting the family, the evangelical church is downsizing due to an exodus of young people who've been the recipients of decades of this targeted programming and attention.

Scripture tells us that children are a gift from God (Ps. 127:3) and describes how faith-filled family relationships should function (Eph. 5:21–33), but the "success" of individual families is not the focus of the Bible's story. Scripture highlights what it is to be a part of a larger community—the people of God, the family of faith. Jesus added perspective to this when he said some family members might betray a believer (Matt. 10:21–22) and demonstrated on the way to the cross how faith might upend and reconfigure the family unit (John 19:25–27). His words call us to sort the idolatry of an idealized family from his invitation to be a part of his family.

Downsizing: Sort It Out

I thought I knew quite a bit about the downsizing process after moving twelve times. But when my husband and I prepared to move for a thirteenth time, cross-country from Chicago to Florida into a 1,000-square-foot mobile home five years ago, we planned on purchasing a new bed, a couple of couches, and a handful of occasional pieces when we arrived. The rest of our

Chapter 7

earthly goods spanning four decades of marriage fit within a single 6′ x 7′ x 8′ shipping container and inside the trunks of our two aging Toyotas.

Prior to that move, we underwent an intense period of sorting and assessing every single one of our possessions. As a matter of course, I'd used our previous moves as an opportunity to selectively edit items we no longer used. But this relocation to a small home in a distant state required a far more radical approach. We did not have the luxury in our new place of warehousing family heirloom furniture, various tchotchke collections, or our assortment of lawnmowers and snow shovels. (I'll confess I wasn't too heartbroken to say good-bye to the shovels.)

The process was clarifying for me. Sentimentality about our possessions was a luxury I could not afford. Sorting through our items to condense them into a small space forced me to name my Norman Rockwell–illustrated dreams of what I once imagined my family's future might look like. Some of those dreams were leftover idols lingering from our homeschool years.

Our fears for our families created an environment in some streams of evangelicalism for a permission structure that allowed the gift of children to become our purpose for being. That idol obscures our ability to respond to a much more difficult message: God has called us all to be his family. God's family includes singles, the disabled, the mentally ill, the addicted, the aged, those navigating dysfunction and generational trauma, the misfits, people from other cultures, people who hold to other political persuasions . . . every tongue, tribe, and nation.

God calls his church the family of God. Jesus emphasized this in his ministry when he said of his disciples, "Here are my mother and my brothers. For whoever does the will of my Father in heaven is my brother and sister and mother" (Matt. 12:49–50). In the early days of the church, believers gathered for fellowship in the temple courts but also met together in homes where they were devoted to deep, meaningful sibling relationships. In Acts 2:42–47 his fol-

Sort It Out

lowers exhibited many of the characteristics of a healthy family. They ate together, shared their possessions, sold their possessions if need be in order to take care of each other, and kept metaphorical empty seats at their tables so they could always welcome new members to their number.

The first commandment of the ten is very clear: we are to have no other gods but the One True God (Exod. 20:3–4). Renouncing our idols is a necessary first step in reordering our relationships. Only then will we be able to hold in tension our fierce love for our children with our membership in the family of God. God's church simply does not have room for our idols. The downsizing that occurs when we repent of our idolatry is essential in rightsizing the church.

Reflect

1. Do you agree that there is an overemphasis on the nuclear or traditional family in evangelicalism? Why or why not?

2. Have you witnessed the effects of dominionism, patriarchy, or the purity message in the evangelical spaces where you've been involved? In your opinion, were those effects positive, negative, or a mix of both?

3. What would a healthy, functional local "church family" look like? How does that description match or differ from the church(es) in your experience?

8

There Are No Shortcuts

In the waning days of Grace Bible Fellowship, an acquaintance who had given our daughter a few guitar lessons called me out of the clear blue one morning at seven o'clock. "I am not in the habit of calling people I don't know very well at this hour," Meg assured me, then began to cry. "But I think the Lord wants me to share this song I wrote with you."

I'm not a morning person, but her words jolted me fully awake. She set down her phone receiver and began to sing:

> Stone by stone, you set to building a church of the
>   man-made kind
> Setting your hearts like hardened stone in the
>   strength of your own mind.
> You're building a house of worship that's made of
>   man's desire.
> Stone by stone it will all come down, it's destined for
>   the fire.
>
> For I know the thoughts I have for you—I would build
>   you up and prosper you,

There Are No Shortcuts

living stones of mercy, tenderness and love.
In the worship of your daily life, put away the petti-
ness of strife
and love, the way the Cornerstone shows the way of
life to you.

In the game of life the cards you're dealt must be
played with utmost care
The stakes are high, and a single lie can catch you
unaware.
A house of cards will always fall—yield your place to
my dear Son
The play of pride will be trumped by love and the
prize you seek is won.

In the words that well from hearts of stone hard-
hearted speech abounds
The foolish woman throws the first stone, and her
house comes tumbling down.
Remember the words I've spoken, seek wisdom from
above,
The woman of wisdom will build her home with healing words of love.

My bride of life will be built of love, all the power will
come from Me,
Step aside and I'll do the work; your part's humility.
Works of obligation and sheer determination
yield stiff-necked, stubborn stones of straw that will
burn up in my fire.[1]

By the time she finished singing, I was crying, too. Meg didn't
know a single thing about the deep division that was tearing apart

1. "Living Stones," by Meg Kausalik, Breadbasket Music, copyright 1997.

Chapter 8

the church. Her call reminded me in a profound way that God wasn't constructing a church building for believers but was creating a living sanctuary from his born-again, Spirit-filled people for his glory, and for the sake of the world.

After Grace Bible Fellowship had its final Sunday morning service a few weeks later, our family found ourselves looking for another new congregational home, which meant again visiting church buildings in search of a gathering of living stones. It would have been far easier at this point to simply abandon the idea of church. Our track record to that point had been marked with one church disaster after another. Yet, Bill and I weren't ready to walk away.

Though we'd heard numerous church leaders use Hebrews 10:24–25 as a shame goad to encourage people not to forsake assembling together by attending weekly church services, at that point, it wasn't the goad that kept us hanging in there. It was the truth of the verse before, Hebrews 10:23: "Let us hold unswervingly to the hope we profess, for he who promised is faithful." We reminded ourselves how often we'd seen goodness as well as disaster. We put our heads together in prayer, asking God to guide us to where our family's living stones might fit next.

It was a long year and a half of wandering, trying one church for a few weeks, then another for a couple of months. Our kids were game, but the search took a toll on all of us.

In January of 2000, a friend invited me to attend a night of worship music at a church we hadn't yet visited. It was a former Bible church that had recently experienced a third wave–style renewal. I was curious about how a church could balance a cessationist past with openness to charismatic expression. Was it the best of both worlds or an ongoing tug-of-war? After Bill and I took some time to evaluate the congregation, we trusted it was more of the former than the latter, and our family plugged into life at Wooded Hills Bible Church.[2]

2. The church has gone through two name changes since we arrived in

There Are No Shortcuts

Even though "Bible church" was in the name, this church's roots weren't in fundamentalism but in conservative mainstream evangelicalism. The group that launched Wooded Hills more than a decade earlier came from a large evangelical megachurch in the area. Despite the drama of the spiritual renewal that had swept through the congregation more recently, it was those megachurch roots that would inform the way the church organized its living stones.

Within a couple of years, Bill had become an elder, and I was hired as a part-time staff member to handle communications. As we became "insiders," we saw how the tools of church growth were being deployed as a way to manage the quickly expanding congregation.

They were tools as familiar to me as the backyard of my childhood home.

When I came to faith in Christ in 1974, nondenominational South Park Church in nearby Park Ridge, Illinois, boasted one of the biggest youth ministries in the area. Youth leaders Bill Hybels and Dave Holmbo had shifted the direction of their programming by asking students what would make the Christian message relevant to them. As a result, Son City was drawing close to a thousand students a week.

Hybels and Holmbo decided to start a church.[3] They spent a month going from door to door conducting a survey. If the respondent already belonged to a local church, they moved on. If not, they asked why the person didn't attend. They heard that people stayed away because they perceived the church was focused on

---

January 2000. They dropped the "Bible" from their name as they moved fully into identifying as a charismatic congregation. They eventually changed the name again and now call themselves Bezalel Church (https://www.bezalelchurch.com/services-3).

3. Holmbo was asked to leave the ministry in 1979 around allegations that he'd abused his power and position with a staff member. The resulting cover-up almost ended the rapidly growing church at that time.

Chapter 8

asking for money, and that services were boring and irrelevant. Hybels and Holmbo developed a target demographic, which eventually became known as Unchurched Harry (and eventually, his wife, Unchurched Mary) to describe the White suburban boomers their new church would target.[4]

One hundred twenty-five Harrys and Marys showed up for the first service of the new church in October 1975 at Willow Creek Theater in Palatine, Illinois.[5] I snuck a couple of visits to the movie-theater-turned-Sunday-morning-church-sanctuary during my high school years. It was entertaining, with great contemporary music—some Christian and some pop standards with spiritually meaningful lyrics, which was a novelty in those days—and earnestly relevant messages designed to show how the Bible applied to my life.

By 1977, the nondenominational church had purchased ninety acres of prime real estate in nearby South Barrington and built a state-of-the-art facility that opened in 1981. Even though Bill and I ended up in other kinds of congregations in the area, Willow Creek's outsized influence couldn't be denied. Churches were either embracing or modifying Willow Creek's seeker-sensitive approach, or they were digging in their heels and denouncing it as "watered down" or "liberal." The fact that Hybels's mentor, the now-disgraced Gilbert Bilezikian, advocated for full inclusion of women in ministry leadership made the church suspect in most conservative evangelical congregations.[6] But those concerns didn't make much of a dent on the church's popular-

4. Joe Engelkemier, "A Church That Draws Thousands," *Ministry*, May 1991, https://tinyurl.com/4xcd93pw.

5. "Bill Hybels," Wikipedia, last edited August 26, 2024, https://tinyurl.com/ann8pe75.

6. In 2020, after Bill Hybels stepped down, credible sexual and power abuse accusations against Gilbert Bilezikian were made public by Hybels's replacement. Steve Warren, "Willow Creek Announces Abuse Allegations

There Are No Shortcuts

ity. By 2000, close to twenty thousand people were attending weekly services.[7]

The pastor at Wooded Hills in Wisconsin admired church management systems and procedures like those being produced by Willow to manage the numerical growth taking place in his congregation. At one point, the staff and leadership team at Wooded Hills took a road trip to attend a church leadership conference at Willow Creek.[8] It was surreal for Bill and me to sit in Willow's state-of-the-art auditorium that was larger than Radio City Music Hall and remember what it was like to visit the megachurch in the 1970s in the old movie-theater days.[9]

Willow had become a worldwide phenomenon due in large part to Hybels's long public romance with the business world. The first two lines of the introduction to his 1995 book *Rediscovering Church: The Story and Vision of Willow Creek Church*, coauthored

---

against Church Co-Founder," CBN, January 29, 2020, https://tinyurl.com/yh932sr4.

7. In 1997, the number in weekly attendance was sixteen thousand ("Talking with . . . a Conversation with Willow Creek's Bill Hybels," Religion News Service, January 1, 1997, https://tinyurl.com/7akh64k9). The church was about to go multisite in 2001: "Big Church Plans TV Branches," *Chicago Tribune*, August 20, 2021, https://tinyurl.com/33sda5ya. By 2015, a couple of years before revelations of Bill Hybels's abuse of power and sexual improprieties became public, the number in weekly attendance was twenty-five thousand ("2015 Largest Participating Churches," Outreach 100, accessed October 4, 2024, https://tinyurl.com/4daez3bm).

8. The Church Leadership Conference was the precursor to the Global Leadership Summit, a worldwide event featuring speakers from business, government, nonprofit innovators, and church leaders focusing on motivating leaders. The Summit was created by a Willow-adjacent organization called the Willow Creek Association.

9. Per the contractor who worked on the sound system for the new auditorium, which was inaugurated in 2004, the 7,200-seat space is 1,200 seats larger than Radio City Music Hall in New York. "Willow Creek Community Church," Danley, accessed October 4, 2024, https://tinyurl.com/26z889sw.

Chapter 8

with his wife, Lynne, are saturated with the kind of language that drove the church's culture: "A few years ago, I called the Willow Creek management team together for a daylong strategic planning session, complete with detailed agenda and outside consultants. Our goal for the day was ambitious, but we could meet it: we meant business."[10] While the anecdote goes on to talk about how the Holy Spirit prompted Hybels to remember that those gathered in that conference room were human beings, not just interchangeable bricks in a rapidly expanding religious empire, the language he used (management team, strategic planning session, detailed agenda, consultants, ambitious, business) captured Hybels's approach to church.

Back in Wisconsin, church leaders at Wooded Hills created org charts, policies, pathways, and rules. We listened to sermons about the leadership skills of Ezra and Nehemiah. The whole congregation studied *The Purpose Driven Life* by another megachurch guru, Rick Warren. Meanwhile, some from the church would travel to various charismatic conferences and gatherings, then return to voice their frustration that Wooded Hills was "quenching the Spirit" because Sunday services were a little more orderly than what they'd experienced somewhere else.

Both sides were battling for control of a congregation in transition. I understood the desires of the brand-new charismatics whose faith had been energized by their power encounters with the Holy Spirit. And as a staff member, I was receiving an up-close tutorial in something I'd first witnessed from a distance since those stolen visits during high school to Willow Creek movie theater: church growth tools deployed to build and manage congregations.

---

10. Bill Hybels and Lynne Hybels, *Rediscovering Church: The Story and Vision of Willow Creek Church* (Grand Rapids: Zondervan, 1995).

There Are No Shortcuts

Turning Stones into Bricks

The church growth movement emerged in the years after World War II. Most credit the work of missionary Donald McGavran, whose 1955 book *The Bridges of God: A Study in the Strategy of Missions* married principles drawn from the social sciences and business to the task of evangelism. He observed that the Western evangelical emphasis on individual decisions for Christ obscured the process by which people groups in other parts of the world and throughout most of history came to faith. He also noted that in cultures hostile to Christianity, individual decisions didn't result in rapid evangelization. To decide for Christ in those settings meant frayed family relationships, social stigma, and possible loss of income, property, or even life. (My own experience after coming to faith in Christ certainly bore that out.)

In the next couple of decades, McGavran's methodology and philosophy influenced those in missions who were committed to begin dismantling the colonialist impulse that still fueled many overseas endeavors. McGavran said that the homogenous nature of relationships in a clan or community could be leveraged by missionaries to Christianize that group, noting, "people become Christian fastest when least change of race or clan is involved."[11] This came to be known as the homogenous unit principle, and was a cornerstone of his call for missionaries to become humble students of the culture/subculture they sought to evangelize, seeking to meet the felt needs of those they hoped to reach with the gospel, sharing the good news in the context of that culture, and planting new churches within those homogenous groupings.

The International Congress on World Evangelization in Lausanne, Switzerland, in 1974 sparked the connection between the work of McGavran and influential theologians like C. Peter Wag-

11. Donald McGavran, *Bridges of God: A Study in the Strategy of Missions* (New York: Friendship, 1955), 23.

Chapter 8

ner and Ralph Winter who sought to grow and strengthen local churches. A number of other scholars and practitioners followed suit, applying McGavran's principles to the challenges of outreach and discipleship in American culture.[12]

By the 1980s, the Jesus freak hippies had traded their 1960s tie-dyed T's and love beads for the three-piece suits and briefcases of business. Secular culture celebrated wealth, excess, and cutthroat business practices in over-the-top TV soap operas like *Dallas* and "reality-based" shows like *Lifestyles of the Rich and Famous*, headlines featuring the antics of ferocious financial warriors like "Queen of Mean" hotelier Leona Helmsley or rising celebrity Donald Trump, and the 1987 movie *Wall Street*, which captured the zeitgeist of the day with the unforgettable line: "Greed, for lack of a better word, is good." The horizon for growth and material success seemed limitless in that era.

While Christians generally seemed to recognize that valorizing greed as a virtue might have been a bridge too far, some evangelical leaders baptized their personal aspirations in the language of growing God's kingdom. After all, the Bible highlighted the explosive numerical growth of the church throughout the book of Acts (2:41, 47; 5:14; 6:1; 9:31; 17:34). To respond to Jesus's call to go make disciples today meant leveraging every modern tool to that end.

An early adopter of church growth methodology was preacher

---

12. On pages 17–18 of his 2010 book *Evaluating the Church Growth Movement: Five Views* (Grand Rapids: Zondervan, 2010), church growth advocate Gary McIntosh cited C. Peter Wagner's courses at Fuller's School of Theology beginning in the mid-1970s on church growth principles as influencing a generation of church growth experts including Elmer Towns, Kent Hunter, John Vaughan, John Maxwell, Rick Warren, Bob Logan, Leither Anderson, Bob Ford, and Eddie Gibbs. John Wimber was involved at Fuller with Wagner until 1978, when he left to plant the first Vineyard congregation. The Fuller program trained over 1,500 people. Some of those men, along with other luminaries in the emerging field, formed the American Society for Church Growth in 1985 in order to disseminate the gospel of business- and science-informed church growth principles.

There Are No Shortcuts

and televangelist Robert Schuller, who focused his positive-thinking message and a marketer's approach to church growth with laser-like precision both locally, in Orange County, California, and nationally (and eventually, internationally) via his *Hour of Power* broadcasts. In 1981, he led the build of the soaring glass Crystal Cathedral, which became a sort of prototype of the evangelical megachurches that would follow over the next years. Schuller wasn't shy about why he thought big. In 2005, he said, "The concept of the mega-church—some have attributed that to me. Whatever people want to buy, they can get it in the shopping center. It's one-stop shopping. Churches should be that way."[13]

Beginning in the 1980s, some churches helmed by young spiritual entrepreneurs like Bill Hybels and Rick Warren at Saddleback Church in southern California who leaned hard on church growth techniques saw their churches became megachurches. The Hartford Institute of Religion Research defines megachurches as congregations drawing more than two thousand people to weekend services.[14] Some of those megachurches grew in following decades to draw exponentially larger crowds. To give a sense of the scale, according to *Outreach* magazine, the ten largest American evangelical congregations in 2023 tabulated over 400,000 people in attendance. The number of these big-box congregations has grown from 350 in 1990 to over 1,400 and counting.[15]

---

13. "We Are Designed to Be Spiritual Creatures," Beliefnet, accessed September 27, 2024, https://tinyurl.com/y4k2kz4n. While Schuller's ministry remained free from the moral failures that have marked too many other megachurch leaders, nevertheless, it could not sustain itself over time. The church's board filed for bankruptcy in 2010, and the Crystal Cathedral was sold to the Diocese of Orange (County) in 2011. ("Christ Cathedral (Garden Grove, California)," Wikipedia, last edited September 7, 2024, https://tinyurl.com/3ph79m3m.) Schuller died at age eighty-eight in 2015.

14. "Megachurch Definition," Hartford Institute for Religion Research, accessed September 27, 2024, https://tinyurl.com/44bwfkbm.

15. Kent Shaffer, "Why Megachurches Keep Growing," Preach It Teach It, accessed September 27, 2024, https://tinyurl.com/599n7dn9.

Chapter 8

With the blessing of church growth teaching, pastors of megachurches evolved into CEOs, evangelism became marketing, and the names of living stones filled uniform brick-shaped slots on an organizational chart in the church conference room. A crop of books and seminars by Christian leadership gurus like John Maxwell promised to unlock the keys to steering the growth of these burgeoning congregations.

Empty Malls

Robert Schuller favorably compared a megachurch to a one-stop shopping center in 2005. However, by that time, the indoor mall was already beginning its decline. In the mid-1980s, there were about 2,500 indoor malls in the United States. By 2023, there were only about 700 still in existence. Some industry analysts estimate that that number will continue to contract to just 250 malls by the end of the 2020s.[16] In a span of just four decades, the glittering promise of one-stop shopping faded as consumer habits changed.

The church growth movement is now in its downsizing era. Books and conferences offering the latest surefire principles are not being produced like they were in the 1980s through the early 2000s. Professor and author Ed Stetzer suggested one core reason for the decline: "The focus became 'growing a church' rather than theological, missional, or evangelistic concerns."[17] Too many weary church leaders saw in church growth materials the promise of being able to apply business principles, sociological insights,

16. Katie Burke and Linda Moss, "Why Retailers Are Abandoning Traditional Malls," *CoStar*, May 22, 2023, https://tinyurl.com/mwcdrr9u.

17. Ed Stetzer, *The Evolution of Church Growth, Church Health, and the Missional Church: An Overview of the Church Growth Movement from, and Back to, Its Missional Roots, Christianity Today* online archive, accessed May 23, 2024, 9.

There Are No Shortcuts

and surefire fixes to the unruly, unpredictable nature of church life in order to build a smoothly functioning organization.

Though the church growth movement began with a focus on outreach and mission, it became for many end users a study in uncritically copying the systems, methods, and techniques promoted by "successful" churches. The message of the kingdom of God got lost in the shuffle. Religion reporter Rick Pidcock observed, "You can't just slap spiritual job titles onto the organizational chart of empire and pretend you're subverting it."[18] Both when I was staff at Wooded Hills and later when I did some freelance communications work with a few churches, I saw many church leaders using org charts to describe how they saw the function of the church. In every case, filling the slots on those charts in order to ensure the work of ministry got done had more to do with keeping the church factory running than it did with utilizing a member's spiritual gifts for the good of the body.

The "well-run" consumer-oriented megachurch did not automatically produce mature disciples. In 2007, leaders at Willow Creek released the results of a study they commissioned to measure if and how its congregants and members of hundreds of other churches connected with its network were growing in their faith. Researchers were surprised to discover that involvement in church activities didn't translate into spiritual maturity, and those who were growing spiritually tended to express growing dissatisfaction and disconnection with the church.[19] While there have always been critics of

18. Rick Pidcock, https://tinyurl.com/2s3985px, accessed October 4, 2024.

19. "What *Reveal* Reveals," editorial, *Christianity Today*, March 2008, https://tinyurl.com/yc7p5sws. Additional resources on this study: "Revealed: What Willow Creek Said Out Loud When It Dared to Look in the Mirror," Christian Leadership Alliance, accessed October 7, 2024, https://tinyurl.com/3ex36p4z; David Fitch, "What Willowcreek's 'Reveal' Reveals: On Just How Difficult (Impossible?) It Is for the Megachurch to Undergo Change," Missio Alliance, November 14, 2007, https://tinyurl.com/yhkhtk97.

Chapter 8

the church growth approach, the *Reveal: Where Are You?* study highlighted from within the megachurch camp some megaproblems.

But the weak approach to disciple making was far from the only problem unfolding in megachurches in the first decades of the twenty-first century. There is a long list of megachurch pastors who have been caught in moral failure or have been accused of abusing their power. And new leaders get added seemingly weekly to this Hall of Shame, joining former church growth success stories Ted Haggard, Mark Driscoll, James MacDonald, Tony Evans, Robert Morris, and Bill Hybels. I learned firsthand at Northwest Suburban Fellowship how the effects of a leader's sin ripple far beyond those at the center of the story, reverberating for years afterward. In a megachurch, the ripples are amplified and stretch far beyond a single church community. Sometimes they stretch around the globe.

Numbers can't measure hurt or loss of faith, but they do capture a story of downsizing. The valuable insights of the *Reveal* study didn't change the heart of the leader at the center of it all, Bill Hybels. In 2015, three years before revelations of founding pastor Bill Hybels's abuse of power and inappropriate relationships with female staffers and congregants, Willow Creek Community Church had over 25,000 people each week attending services. In 2023, there were around 7,000 in attendance.[20]

Downsizing: There Are No Shortcuts

I once heard a folksy preacher say, "You can do it God's way ... or you can do it God's way." He wasn't being redundant. Instead, he was

20. Summary of Bill Hybels's downfall and the numbers that reflect the effect it has had on attendance: Kate Shellnutt, "Willow Creek Investigation: Allegations against Bill Hybels Are Credible," *Christianity Today*, February 28, 2019, https://tinyurl.com/mv5xchae; Abby Perry, "Willow Creek and Harvest Struggle to Move On," *Christianity Today*, February 13, 2020, https://tinyurl.com/2vper7r8; Dave Dummitt, "Willow Creek Community Church," Outreach 100, accessed October 7, 2024, https://tinyurl.com/4c5bschn.

There Are No Shortcuts

trying to emphasize that there are no shortcuts to obedience, nor can the work be outsourced. His point was that it is better to choose obedience in the first place, but if we don't, the One who loves us enough to discipline us when we choose our own way will continue to call us to return to him via correction and consequences.

There are no shortcuts to building the church, nor to downsizing her. The temple in Jerusalem was made of stones created by God, hewn at the quarry, and transported to the construction site to be fitted into place (1 Kings 6:7). No human-made, uniform bricks were used for the holy structure. Those living in the first century would have immediately understood the metaphor used by both Paul (Eph. 2:19-22) and Peter (1 Pet. 2:4-5): the church is a sanctuary under construction, built from living stones fitted together by God himself. Our attempts to build churches using assembly-line-produced bricks miss this key difference. Certainly people came to faith and grew spiritually in megachurches, but I believe it was despite the church model at the foundation, not because of it.

Former "successful" megachurch pastor Eugene Kim found himself asking questions of the modern models for church and is now investing his life in spurring others to step into a downsized, hopeful future. He suggested, "One baby step toward change. . . . Acknowledge that most of the practices and structures of our prevailing model of institutional 'church' are rooted in industry and Western culture, not anything biblical or theological. That means we can expand our imaginations and ask deeper questions about what 'church' is and what it's for. We can dream, experiment, and create new things. The way it's done is not the way it has to be."[21]

"The way it's done" in wide swaths of evangelicalism has long drawn its inspiration from what's worked in business, education, and entertainment. Baked into the DNA of evangelicalism are the values of conversionism (the belief that each individual needs to

---

21. Eugene Kim, X post, February 23, 2024, https://tinyurl.com/4za cu2zm. Kim is one of the facilitators of the newwinecollective.com.

Chapter 8

be born again) and activism (outreach through mission and social reform efforts). Before the church growth movement took hold, many evangelicals were seeking to draw crowds to gospel presentations via meeting felt needs and through celebrity appearances. For instance, in the nineteenth century, Sunday schools offered an on-ramp to education for the children of poor and working-class parents. These schools taught many children to read while giving them instruction in basic Christian doctrine. In the early years of the twentieth century, former baseball player Billy Sunday used his fame in popular culture to attract people to his rallies, where he would then preach a message about salvation.

The church growth movement blended those impulses to draw a crowd and meet a need with sophisticated modern tools; churches consequently outsourced their reason for being, leaning on marketing instead of evangelism and offering church-based programs that easily devolved into busywork. Evangelicals have learned to build better bricks.

But God has never chosen to use mass-produced bricks to build his church. Downsizing means we will leave our brick-making skills behind us and recognize that he's always and only built his church from living stones, on the cornerstone of his beloved Son.

Reflect

1. Have you ever visited or been a regular attender at a megachurch? If so, what did you most appreciate about it? What left you with concerns or questions?
2. Should modern disciplines such as business, science, and sociology inform the way in which we think about a downsized church as we look forward to the future? What role, if any, might these things play?
3. Willow Creek's 2007 *Reveal* study showed that involvement in church activities didn't automatically lead to spiritual maturity while also highlighting that those who were maturing spiri-

There Are No Shortcuts

tually were often increasingly dissatisfied with their church experience. Have those findings been borne out in your experience? What might this tell us about where downsizing in evangelicalism might lead?

9

Saying Good-bye to Useless Things

Bill, our three teen kids, and I had been packed together on a charter bus for fourteen hours with about forty other members from Wooded Hills Bible Church. We then spent a restless overnight in a one-star Washington, DC, hotel before awakening before dawn to make our way to the Capitol Mall the morning of September 2, 2000. We'd come to answer a call. Specifically, we'd come to DC to answer The Call.

We emerged onto the historic green and located the area marked "Wisconsin," one of many areas set aside by The Call DC organizers for groups from each state. When we got to our assigned location, I settled onto a patch of weedy, matted grass to survey the scene. There was a giant stage with the Capitol building forming a backdrop behind it, and a few Jumbotrons positioned down the mall so those far from the action could still see and participate. As the tech crew ran a few final sound checks, the buzz of anticipation rippled through the growing crowd as the sun began its ascent in the eastern sky. The Mall quickly filled with around 400,000 people who'd converged in that space for a day of prayer,

Saying Good-bye to Useless Things

fasting, worship, and repentance.[1] We'd come to pray for families, our churches, the world, and especially for our nation that was just two months away from a presidential election.

As I noted in the previous chapter, Wooded Hills Bible Church had a combustible mix of church growth proponents and passionate charismatics restless for a stream of unfiltered mountaintop spiritual experiences. In the late summer of 2000, church leaders were trying to balance the desires of both constituencies, which is how a busload of people from Wooded Hills found ourselves in DC arming for spiritual battle.

We'd come because a number of influencers at the church brought news about a solemn assembly being convened by Lou Engle, who had a growing reputation in charismatic circles as a "John the Baptist–style prophetic intercessor."[2] His message to the church? Our country was on the precipice of destruction, and we needed to go full Joel 2, which meant convening a solemn assembly at the seat of power. Inspired by a prayer gathering sponsored by parachurch men's organization Promise Keepers on the Capitol Mall in 1997, Engle began dreaming of a similar gathering that would include men and women, old and young. He partnered with Pasadena-based pastor Che Ahn, and soon word of the event was ricocheting through the charismatic grapevine, at that time, a network of loosely affiliated churches, ministries, conferences, and media outlets. Interestingly, when I talked with noncharismatic evangelical friends ahead of our trip, not one had ever heard of this big event. It would take another decade and a half before the

---

1. US Park Service estimates placed the crowd size at 400,000: "Lou Engle: Answering The Call in D.C.," CBN, December 10, 2022, https://tiny url.com/mpsh75sb.

2. Shawn Akers, "Lou Engle Sees Another Jesus Movement Rising," *Charisma*, March 9, 2016, https://tinyurl.com/3decye8n.

Chapter 9

rest of the church—and the world—would begin to recognize the strength and effectiveness of this network.

The platform program began at dawn with what has since become a familiar sight at Christian political events—a handful of Messianic Jews alongside gentile Christian Zionists, wearing tallit (prayer shawls) and yarmulkes (head coverings), gathered to blow shofars (rams' horns, used in worship during Rosh Hashanah services) to sanctify the gathering and serve as a spiritual call to arms. "That must make you feel good," someone from our group whispered to me. Actually, it left me queasy. I understood the intent of this display, but it felt to me like Jewish cosplay rather than a spiritually meaningful act.[3]

Raspy-voiced event organizer Lou Engle emceed the day, which focused on intergenerational reconciliation (turning the hearts of the fathers to the children and children to the fathers in the spirit of Malachi 4:6), praying for an end to abortion and sexual licentiousness, asking God to send young missionaries into the world, and rallying prayer support so our nation would return to God. No one mentioned that this meant electing Republican George W. Bush, but by this point in evangelical history, I think most people on the Mall that day understood that there was only one political party who shared "our" values.

Speakers included revivalist author Dr. Michael Brown; Campus Crusade for Christ/Cru founder Dr. Bill Bright; pastor Che Ahn; televangelist Benny Hinn; Daryl Scott, the father of slain Columbine, Colorado, student Rachel Scott; a mix of younger rising starts in the prayer movement who offered prayers; and a rotating cast of musicians leading us in sung worship, including Michael W. Smith and Jason Upton.

---

3. For more on the problem of Christian appropriation of Jewish symbols, see Michelle Van Loon, "Appropriating Jewish Religious Symbols May Not Communicate What Christians Think It Does," *Christ and Pop Culture*, September 6, 2022, https://tinyurl.com/262vzza5.

Saying Good-bye to Useless Things

The morning was full of energy and passion as we sang, wept, repented, and did spiritual battle on behalf of our fallen country. By midafternoon, the weather had turned inclement, and the crowd of 400,000 began to thin. Our group joined them. We boarded our bus and headed back to Wisconsin, exhausted but sure that this day was going to change history. In retrospect, I don't recall anyone expressing a vision for exactly how a transformed, revived culture would look, other than "the opposite of what we have now."

A year later, nearly to the day, when the Twin Towers and Pentagon were attacked by Al-Qaeda terrorists, there was a rising urgency to call the country back to God in many circles. A year and half after that, some of the young people who were on that mall found themselves on a different kind of battlefield—this time in Iraq, sent there by claims that Iraqi leader Saddam Hussein had assisted Al-Qaeda and what turned out to be false reports of weapons of mass destruction.

We were at war. But evangelicals had been in spiritual basic training for decades. To be a good soldier of the cross in our circles at the time meant recognizing that there was no going AWOL from the state of spiritual warfare in which we all lived.

Scripture has highlighted the spiritual conflict between God and the rebel created being, Satan, and his allies that has existed in our world since Eden.[4] Through her history, the church has wrestled with what it means to be engaged in spiritual warfare. This has netted everything from extreme ascetic practices meant to vanquish sinful flesh to religiously fueled "holy wars" ostensibly waged to win more territory for Team Christendom. Eastern Orthodox, Catholic, and some Protestant denominations include a renun-

---

4. A few examples of spiritual warfare in Scripture include Gen. 3; Exod. 7-12; 1 Sam. 16:14; 1 Chron. 21:1; Job 1-2; Isa. 14:12-20; Matt. 8:28-34; 12:22-29; Mark 8:31-33; Luke 4:1-13; Acts 16:16-18; 1 Thess. 2:18; and the book of Revelation.

Chapter 9

ciation of Satan and his works in baptismal vows. Many modern evangelicals have heard some form of teaching on spiritual warfare featuring Paul's words in 2 Corinthians 10:4–6 and Ephesians 6.

But the text that formed evangelical understanding of the topic was penned in 1986 by Assemblies of God minister Frank Peretti. His supernatural novel *This Present Darkness* and its 1989 sequel, *Piercing the Darkness*, have been the foundation of the way many believers understand spiritual warfare. The books portray the intense conflict between angels and demons happening all around the people of a small town. In 2006, *Christianity Today* magazine created a list of the top fifty books that have shaped evangelicals. *This Present Darkness* clocked in at #34 on the list, along with this bit of commentary: "InterVarsity Press editor Al Hsu says Peretti's horror thriller 'challenged evangelicals to take spiritual warfare and the supernatural seriously.' Maybe, in some cases, too seriously."[5]

Peretti's imagined world of evil conspiracies made the invisible real for a generation of readers. A 2022 *Vox* article noted, "Peretti, who went on to write far more allegorical novels, most likely meant much of this fantasy to be read metaphorically, not literally. But his audience missed that memo. He engaged his readers so completely that the *Darkness* duology stayed on bestseller lists for nearly a decade."[6]

The books spawned a host of spiritual warfare books, conferences, and newly minted deliverance experts across evangelicalism. There was a heavy concentration of materials written by and for charismatics and Pentecostals who had long been armed and ready to do battle with demons.[7]

5. "Top 50 Books That Have Shaped Evangelicals," *Christianity Today*, October 2006, https://tinyurl.com/y82y9jk7.

6. Aja Romano, Alissa Wilkinson, and Emily St. James, "Revisiting the Christian Fantasy Novels That Shaped Decades of Conservative Hysteria," *Vox*, April 28, 2022, https://tinyurl.com/3txyvn2b.

7. Books popular in mainstream evangelicalism included Neil Ander-

Saying Good-bye to Useless Things

A lot of the activity in the charismatic churches we circulated in during the late 1990s and early 2000s took its cues from *This Present Darkness* rather than the Bible. I heard one person praying publicly against an evil spirit deemed responsible for hot flashes, and spent time among those who worried obsessively about speaking forth only positive confession "words of life" lest they bring a curse upon themselves. The latter was a mingling of Word of Faith teaching with popular understanding of spiritual warfare. There was a functional dualism at play in those circles, as if the world was caught up in a long war between two equal competitors, God and Satan, facing off in a mixed martial arts match. Believers were looking for an inside track on Satan's schemes as a shortcut to spiritual authority.[8]

The focus on spiritual warfare and gatherings like The Call DC were connected to a movement that emerged in the charismatic world just offstage of mainstream evangelicalism in the waning decades of the last century. It drew from a variety of wells, including the Latter Rain and Healing revivals of midcentury Pentecostalism, the Shepherding movement of second-wave charismatic renewal, the signs and wonders experiences that fueled the third-wave Vineyard movement, Dominion theology, and a hyperfocus on spiritual warfare. It was a web of relationships that changed the way many charismatic churches and ministries related to one another, and it shifted the way in which spiritual authority was exercised.

---

son's *The Bondage Breaker* and Mark Bubeck's *Preparing for Battle* (1999). While deliverance ministry had been a mainstay in Pentecostal and charismatic circles from their beginnings, the Peretti books fanned the flames of interest, and authors like Derek Prince (*They Shall Expel Demons*, published 1998) and Apostle John Eckhart, who self-published his own guides to spiritual warfare and deliverance, produced material to address the hunger for more information that was stirred by Peretti's work.

8. A representative sample of passages expressing reliance on God in times of physical or spiritual battle: Exod. 14:14; Deut. 20:4; 2 Chron. 20:14; Ps. 34:17; Luke 10:19; James 4:7; and 1 John 4:4.

Chapter 9

It may have started offstage, but it ended up in the spotlight in American politics beginning in 2015.

Enter Stage Far Right: The New Apostolic Reformation

Independent Network Charismatic Christianity, which has become popularly known as the New Apostolic Reformation (NAR), is a movement based on claims of spiritual authority and exercises of spiritual power. It emerged from the belief that spiritual authority for the church didn't belong in the old hierarchies found in local congregations or denominations. Instead, the biblical order prescribed that authority belonged to those with the "fivefold" spiritual leadership gifts mentioned in Ephesians 4:11-13: "So Christ himself gave the apostles, the prophets, the evangelists, the pastors and teachers, to equip his people for works of service, so that the body of Christ may be built up until we all reach unity in the faith and in the knowledge of the Son of God and become mature, attaining to the whole measure of the fullness of Christ."

In previous chapters, I've touched on C. Peter Wagner's influence in missions, in the launch of the Vineyard, and in church growth teachings. But he has also been a key figure in the teaching regarding how the NAR would return the church to its intended first-century structure, thus allowing it to access both spiritual and temporal power. He said, "It is a 'reformation' because we are currently witnessing the most radical change in the way of 'doing church' since the Protestant Reformation. It is 'apostolic' because the recognition of the gift and office of apostle is the most radical of a whole list of changes from the old wineskin. It is 'new' to distinguish it from several older traditional church groups that have incorporated the term 'apostolic' into their official name."[9]

9. C. Peter Wagner, *Apostles Today: Biblical Government for Biblical Power* (Bloomington, MN: Chosen Books, 2006).

Saying Good-bye to Useless Things

This network of apostles and prophets is mostly self-appointed, then validated by others in the movement, according to researchers Brad Christerson and Richard Flory: "Leaders in the moment would say that people are recognized as apostles because of the influence that they have—not only over your own congregation but over other leaders. But there's definitely a good deal of self-appointing going on. Peter Wagner, a leader in the New Apostolic Reformation movement, referred to himself as a 'super apostle,' because he was influential with a bunch of other apostles."[10]

There's no denying Wagner's influence, but many other leaders in this network also speak with authority to adherents. Wagner's Apostolic Council of Prophetic Elders has included many other influencers in the NAR orbit over the last two decades, including intercessor Cindy Jacobs; ministry leader Rick Joyner; missionary Heidi Baker; pastors Bill Hamon, Dutch Sheets, Paula White, and Loren Sandford; prophetic voices Chuck Pierce and Jim Goll; worship leader Sean Feucht; and broadcaster Lance Wallnau. Public figures who've expressed public support for NAR ideas or shared a stage at NAR conferences or gatherings include former vice presidential candidate Sarah Palin, retired general Michael Flynn, Speaker of the House Mike Johnson, and Representatives Marjorie Taylor Greene and Paul Gosar.

Originally, the NAR was a loose network of generally like-minded churches and ministries, but it has coalesced around Republican political involvement. This network now has leaders, momentum, and direction. While no single creed or doctrinal statement captures the belief system of all adherents, most in NAR circles would affirm:

---

10. Bob Smietana, "The 'Prophets' and 'Apostles' Leading the Quiet Revolution in American Religion," *Christianity Today*, August 3, 2017, https://tinyurl.com/yckak69f.

Chapter 9

- *Spiritual authority rests in individuals, not church structure.* Often first self-appointed, the leaders of this movement have been affirmed as evangelists, pastors, teachers, apostles, or prophets, though it is those wearing the mantle of prophet or apostle that provide direction and exercise authority.[11] Some scholars have noted that the NAR power structure that resides primarily in individuals exercising spiritual authority over networks of congregations and ministries bears more than a passing resemblance to the Shepherding movement of the 1970s.[12]
- *Spiritual mapping is the battle strategy.* In 1991, researcher George Otis Jr. developed the notion of creating a spiritual profile of a particular community or area for the purposes of targeted, specific, strategic "warfare" prayer as part of a mission effort. By identifying specific dark spirits that seemed to have control in a region, mapping proponents believed their prayers could break through demonic strongholds and lead to transformation. C. Peter Wagner taught classes on the practice at Fuller Seminary in the 1990s. Interestingly, Otis was quoted in a 1998 *Christianity Today* article noting that spiritual mapping had more traction at that time among mainstream evangelicals than it did in the charismatic community.[13] Even as he spoke those words, that was changing fast. It was for many in the NAR world a great big weapon in their spiritual warfare arsenal. Praying against "territorial spirits" over various cities and

11. Many mainstream evangelicals believe there haven't been any apostles since the last of the apostles named in Scripture died, but those in Pentecostal and charismatic circles believe those that guide networks of churches with supernatural insight have the spiritual gift of apostle because all the gifts named in Scripture belong to the church today.

12. David Moore, referenced in John Weaver, *The New Apostolic Reformation: History of a Modern Charismatic Movement* (Jefferson, NC: McFarland & Co., 2016), Kindle location 2910.

13. Art Moore, "Spiritual Mapping Gains Credibility among Leaders," *Christianity Today*, January 12, 1998, https://tinyurl.com/3n7jzdxe.

Saying Good-bye to Useless Things

nations was standard practice at charismatic church services and prayer gatherings by the time we went to The Call DC.

• *Seven Mountain Mandate is the end game.* In 1975, Loren Cunningham of Youth with a Mission and Bill Bright, the head of Campus Crusade for Christ (Cru), met to share a vision each man believed God had given him. Those visions were astonishingly similar. Each called for believers to exercise their God-given authority over what they identified as the seven mountains (or pillars) of society for kingdom purposes. These mountains were religion, family, education, government, media, entertainment, and business.[14] The Seven Mountain Mandate was repackaged Dominionism for the nascent NAR movement in the waning days of the last century, and it took on a life of its own as it gained unprecedented access to political power in 2015.

It was heady stuff for many in the NAR orbit to have their trusted leaders unfolding prayer strategies, taking on demonic strongholds, and sharing prophetic "insider information" promising access to power on those seven mountains. Nowhere was this more evident than on the mountain of government.[15] As Donald Trump, dubbed by some a "modern-day Cyrus" (an unbelieving Babylonian king whose reign was used by God to return the chosen people to their land),[16] moved toward the Republican nomination in 2016, there was a virtual torrent of prophetic declarations

14. "The Seven Mountains of Societal Influence," Generals International, accessed September 27, 2024, https://tinyurl.com/3dxd96x6.

15. [Terry Gross], "A Leading Figure in the New Apostolic Reformation," NPR, October 3, 2011, https://tinyurl.com/5n6zx48p.

16. For additional explanation about this biblical reference: Katherine Stewart, "Why Trump Reigns as King Cyrus," *New York Times*, December 31, 2018, https://tinyurl.com/2ur75suh; Tara Isabella Burton, "The Biblical Story the Christian Right Uses to Defend Trump," *Vox*, March 5, 2018, https://tinyurl.com/4etm8s8s.

Chapter 9

in support of this candidacy. These ranged from the amplification of firefighter Mark Taylor's 2011 prophecy about a Trump presidency, daily Defcon Code Red prayer alerts and calls from various NAR leaders, and groups within the network showing up to pray for or participate in Trump's political rallies. During his presidency, Donald Trump's faith advisory team was composed of mainstream evangelical culture-war stalwarts like James Dobson, pastor Robert Jeffress, and organizer Ralph Reed, along with NAR-aligned preachers/speakers like Rodney Howard-Browne, Paula White, and Robert Morris.[17]

Decades of basic training in culture warring and spiritual battles created an environment hospitable to the syncretized "faith" in power known as Christian nationalism that was championed by the NAR, as well as celebrated in many sectors of mainstream evangelicalism. Christian nationalism is the idea that our laws and social order must reflect the belief that America, the world's "city on a hill," was founded as a Christian nation.[18]

It wasn't surprising to me that spiritual warfare became physical combat when some who'd been involved in "Jericho Prayer March" activities protesting the election of Joe Biden made their way to a prayer rally in Washington the morning of January 6,

17. Adelle M. Banks, "The Key Evangelical Players on Trump's Advisory Board," *National Catholic Reporter*, September 5, 2017, https://tinyurl.com/4s9chufw.

18. As of this writing, the story of the rise in Christian nationalism in evangelicalism is continuing to unfold. Some relevant reading on the topic include Pew Research's statistical snapshot of the movement ("Christianity's Place in Politics, and 'Christian Nationalism,'" Pew Research Center, March 15, 2024, https://tinyurl.com/2kv4k6kd); David French's *New York Times* op-ed ("What Is Christian Nationalism, Exactly?" *New York Times*, February 25, 2024, https://tinyurl.com/mvv5t24h); Tim Alberta's *The Kingdom, the Power, and the Glory: American Evangelicals in an Age of Extremism*; Andrew Whitehead's *American Idolatry: How Christian Nationalism Betrays the Gospel and Threatens the Church*; and filmmaker Rob Reiner's 2024 documentary (*God and Country*).

Saying Good-bye to Useless Things

2021.[19] There's no way to tell exactly how many of those at the prayer rally joined the insurrectionist mob that stormed the Capitol building, but judging by the chants, prayers, and declarations of those inside the building that afternoon, it is safe to say that some were present because they'd been influenced by NAR teaching, prayer events, and relationships.[20]

The Call DC in 2000 was the high-water mark of my personal involvement in the NAR world, though it would be four more years before we left Wisconsin and Wooded Hills Bible Church. As our kids began to leave the nest, Bill and I agreed that our sojourn in Wisconsin was at an end. We returned to Illinois, first moving into a small rental townhome in a northern suburb of Chicago that was less than half the size of our Wisconsin home. The move caused us to rid ourselves of a shocking amount of stuff we realized we no longer needed. It was our first significant round of downsizing, both physically and spiritually.

The quiet of our downsized life gave me space to reflect on my years as a private in the evangelical army before I was sent by my charismatic leaders to the front lines of nonstop spiritual battle. I didn't realize until I left that environment how physically and emotionally depleted I was by the hype of a nonstop barrage of existential threats and the hyperspiritualized quest for earthly power. I understood that my fellow Christian soldiers were striving for control in an out-of-control modern world. I recognized that desire for control in myself, amplified by the lingering effects of spiritual abuse, drew my soul for far too long to one spiritual battle after another.

19. Thomas Lecaque, "The Twisted, Trumpist Religion of Jan. 6th," *Bulwark*, January 6, 2022, https://tinyurl.com/2p8mwvyc.

20. A couple of examples: Christina Zhao, "Florida Pastor and Son Arrested in Capitol Riot after Congregant Provided Evidence to FBI," *Newsweek*, June 26, 2021, https://tinyurl.com/5n8eps3x; Dan Sullivan, "Palm Harbor Messianic Rabbi Gets House Arrest, Probation in Jan. 6 Capitol Breach," *Tampa Bay Times*, January 20, 2022, https://tinyurl.com/yc6ejmuu.

Chapter 9

After our move, I finally found my way to a counselor to begin processing the trauma of spiritual abuse and grieving the deaths of both of my parents. Downsizing gave me the gift of space to reflect and mourn. Bill and I quietly made our exit from worshiping in the charismatic world. We continued to stay in touch with people we considered friends from previous churches, both in person and via social media. Those exchanges had been focused on family updates or sharing what was happening in their congregations.

But almost every single one of them had shifted directions like a well-trained group of synchronized swimmers by 2015. They were now posting urgent political "prophecies" from NAR voices, sharing wild conspiracy theories, and passing on "news" from dubious sources like the *Epoch Times*, which was funded by the non-Christian Falun Gong cult. Several people came after us with the zeal of revivalists seeking to pull us from the brink of hell by converting us to Trumpism. I remembered when they used to talk about Jesus. Maybe they thought they still were, but all that came out of their mouths was far-right politics and increasingly paranoid, occasionally antisemitic conspiracy theories. The NAR, and similar political groups in the noncharismatic world, has offered adherents what the military promises: purpose, mission, bonhomie, and the opportunity to be a part of something bigger than themselves.

Downsizing: Saying Good-bye to Useless Things

It is humbling to recognize that maybe you've invested a lot of time and money into something with little lasting value. Downsizing forces that kind of reckoning with the truth. When I've assisted others in emptying the house of a deceased relative in preparation for a sale, there are usually sobering existential moments when I realize how much energy was once expended in collecting that teacup collection that no one in the family is interested in inheriting. Certainly, for the collector, there were many moments of

Saying Good-bye to Useless Things

pleasure and discovery. But for the downsizers, there is simply the work of disposal, either by finding a buyer for the collection, hauling it to Goodwill or the Salvation Army, or, as a last resort, sending the whole lot to the recycling center.

The notion of the evangelical church as an army of spiritual and cultural warriors has been fed by many different tributaries. It is like a collection that has been curated over time out of ideas that may not seem to have anything in common at first glance, but is forged in the desire for power and control that resides in each of us. Downsizing in this case is going to take more than reassessing the impact of Frank Peretti books on the evangelical imagination or distancing ourselves from NAR teaching. The rise of Christian nationalism has the imprint of so many familiar teachings to which I've been exposed in majority-White evangelicalism over the last fifty years: authoritarianism, prosperity teaching, centering of the traditional family, patriarchy, dispensational theology, spiritual and cultural war posturing, and revivalism, all funneled into political action. Years ago, I was warned about the dreaded "slippery slope" of leftist moral compromise that would turn America into a lawless, hedonistic land. At the time, no one seemed to recognize that it was possible for many evangelicals to slide down the slippery slope in the opposite direction.

History is filled with the unhappy accounts of what happens when the church pursues worldly power. These stories have the same ending every time: the community of faith faces a painful, often-bloody reckoning. We recognize this, yet this desire to rule is not easily uprooted from our souls. The promise of power was one of the three core human temptations Jesus faced in the wilderness (Matt. 4:8–10; Luke 4:5–8). We have learned to clothe the will to power in military garb and call it spiritual warfare. The real battleground isn't up there atop those seven mountains. It's much closer to home.

The hunger for dominion is at the heart of so much bad practice in the church and has overflowed in the ways in which many

Chapter 9

self-identifying evangelicals express themselves in American culture. We in the church can choose humility before God, or we will likely have it chosen for us in coming years. The net result of either option will be downsizing.

The hymn captured in Philippians 2:5–11 names our remedy:

> In your relationships with one another, have the same mindset
> as Christ Jesus:
> > Who, being in very nature God,
> > > did not consider equality with God
> > > > something to be used to his own advantage;
> > rather, he made himself nothing
> > > by taking the very nature of a servant,
> > > being made in human likeness.
> > And being found in appearance as a man,
> > > he humbled himself
> > > by becoming obedient to death—even death on
> > > > a cross!
> > Therefore God exalted him to the highest place
> > > and gave him the name that is above every name,
> > that at the name of Jesus every knee should bow,
> > > in heaven and on earth and under the earth,
> > and every tongue acknowledge that Jesus Christ
> > > is Lord,
> > > to the glory of God the Father.

History tells us we will be dealing with our longing to rule as long as we're in this world.

If a rummage sale is in progress in the church, it will demand a reckoning with our human desire for power and control. May it lead us to honest ongoing examen about its effects on leaders and followers alike. May it remind us that God called his church to be peacemakers, not an army. May it lead us to embrace humility,

Saying Good-bye to Useless Things

and free us to learn the way of Jesus like the born-again children he's calling us to become.

Reflect

1. How do you understand the notion of spiritual warfare? How does that understanding align with and differ from what you've seen taught in the evangelical congregations of which you've been a part?
2. One of the core ideas of those aligned with the NAR is that spiritual authority rests in individuals, not church structure. While this has led to the elevation of personalities and the abuse of power, the question remains of what church governance and humble leadership might look like in the future. What are your thoughts about the enduring value of existing denominational and congregational structures and pathways to leadership within those structures?
3. How have you navigated your own relationship to power and authority in the church?

10

Freedom in Leaving Most Everything Behind

Bill and I remembered the long, long commutes he faced in the Chicago metropolitan area the last time we lived there. When we returned to the area in 2004, we chose a temporary landing spot based on balancing what we could afford with sane drive times to his workplace. As a result, we transplanted into northern suburban soil that was Chicagoland-familiar yet brand-new to us. Bill was finishing a master's degree at Trinity Evangelical Divinity School in Deerfield while he continued his full-time career in tech. I ended up getting a part-time job at the university bookstore, which gave me access to all the books I could wish to read (which turned out to be a lot!) and connected me with a lot of interesting thinkers and ideas that began to give me perspective on some of the hair-raising experiences we'd had in our various churches to date.

Beginning in the late 1990s, a variety of writers, pastors, and speakers started interrogating both theology and practice within evangelicalism—early adopters of the faith-deconstruction process. These early adopters came to be known as the Emergent church (or conversation, depending on whom you asked). This

Freedom in Leaving Most Everything Behind

conversation signaled the beginning of an initial round of downsizing within evangelicalism. Author Peter DeHaan described the Emergent conversation as "an effort to reclaim church practices from a biblical perspective to reform them to be relevant in a postmodern culture."[1] This impulse toward reformation or deconstruction might have been true of at least some evangelicals in the Emergent church stream, but not all. Some had moved beyond evangelicalism into the theologically and culturally progressive mainline world. Others walked away from religion entirely.

Some who came to be identified with the Emergent stream included author Brian McLaren, whose 2001 book *A New Kind of Christian: A Tale of Two Friends on a Spiritual Journey* gave voice to the kinds of questions many younger evangelicals were asking, along with megachurch pastor Rob Bell, philosopher Peter Rollins, theologian Tony Jones, former youth leader Donald Miller, and, for a while, shock-jock pastor Mark Driscoll.

During this same period, in part as a reaction to the Emergent conversation, a neo-Reformed movement sprung up within evangelicalism, spearheaded by Trinity Evangelical Divinity School professor D. A. Carson and the late Tim Keller, pastor of Redeemer Presbyterian in New York City. Dubbed the Gospel Coalition, these men were joined by conservative Calvinist preaching luminaries including John Piper, C. J. Mahaney, Josh Harris, and, after he edged away from the Emergent crew, Mark Driscoll.[2] I was working at Trinity during the early years of the Gospel Coalition and

---

1. Peter DeHaan. "What Happened to the Emergent Church?," Peter dehaan.com, April 13, 2022, https://tinyurl.com/3ndhs4tn.

2. Mahaney was the head of a network of charismatic Reformed churches (Sovereign Grace Ministries) until 2013. At that time, he was facing allegations that he'd covered up allegations of sexual abuse in the ministry. The statute of limitations prevented the case from going forward. Tiffany Stanley, "The Sex-Abuse Scandal That Devastated a Suburban Megachurch," *Washingtonian*, February 14, 2016, https://tinyurl.com/ps58v2kv. Josh Harris, the author of *I Kissed Dating Goodbye*, was his protégé in the ministry.

Chapter 10

saw many seminary students drawn to the movement best described by the adjectives in the title of a 2008 book by Trinity student Collin Hansen: *Young, Restless, Reformed: A Journalist's Journey with the New Calvinists*. I was never an adherent, because the group tended to court periodic controversy with a combative approach to drawing Reformed theological lines in the sand, its complementarianism, and its embrace of some leaders with a history of abuse or cover-up. But they seemed to do just fine without my participation. The Gospel Coalition's conferences and websites have influenced huge numbers of conservative Reformed believers in the United States and around the world for nearly two decades.

In the middle of the new century's first decade, the things I was reading and the conversations I was having at work told me I wasn't alone with my questions. One big one to which I returned: Why was I still bothering with church after all our family had been through to this point? The noble-sounding response to this question would be to echo what Peter said when many of Jesus's fans stopped following him: "You do not want to leave too, do you?" Jesus asked the Twelve.

"Simon Peter answered him, 'Lord, to whom shall we go? You have the words of eternal life. We have come to believe and to know that you are the Holy One of God'" (John 6:67–69).

Yet I've been acquainted with quite a few people who'd affirmed Peter's words and had chosen to opt out of a church life that obscured their view of Jesus. Believe me, Bill and I considered joining them.

I knew well from my teen years what it was to practice my faith in isolation. I believed God drew near to people who weren't free to gather with other believers due to issues like persecution, illness, or caregiving responsibilities. I believed he was near to those who loved him but left the church because clergy had abused their power, violated their trust, and broken their hearts.

Even in hyperindividualized evangelical culture, I couldn't escape the fact that church wasn't about me, but we. I'd witnessed

Freedom in Leaving Most Everything Behind

a lot of terrible behavior from church leaders, but I'd also seen self-giving love at work in the church communities of which we'd been a part: believers showing up to clean the toilets of someone who'd had surgery, caring for the children of impoverished single mothers who worked the night shift, offering financial help in the face of sudden job loss, weeping with those who wept and rejoicing with those who rejoiced. Pastor Dietrich Bonhoeffer said, "The church is the church only when it exists for others. . . . The church must share in the secular problems of ordinary human life, not dominating, but helping and serving. It must tell men of every calling, what it means to live in Christ, to exist for others."[3] I had witnessed enough scenes of the church being the church, and when she was, she was breathtakingly beautiful. I still believed the church was out there. She would never fit neatly into the institutional containers human beings created for her, but neither was she entirely absent from many of those containers.

Those containers—the institutional church—function for many believers as a school. We gather to learn the way of Jesus from our life together in ways we can't or don't on our own. And so, Bill and I stepped once again into the classroom in 2006.

School Days

After Bill and I purchased a small home in a far northern suburb of Chicago in 2006, we began attending a congregation that was grounded in formal, preevangelical church forms. It turns out that we were not the only low-church evangelicals that were finding our way into those pews.

We landed in an Anglican church plant whose origins were connected to the founding of the Anglican Mission in America in 2000. The Mission was created in reaction to the Episcopal Church and

---

3. Dietrich Bonhoeffer, *Letters and Papers from Prison* (New York: Simon & Schuster, 2011), 382.

Chapter 10

Anglican Church of Canada approving LGBTQ+ clergy and being willing to perform weddings for same-sex couples. A couple of African Anglican bishops agreed to provide oversight to a theologically conservative group that wanted to separate from these two church bodies while still remaining part of the global Anglican Communion. This division was reframed as a new mission. Most of the churches in that mission ended up becoming part of a new denomination led by North American leadership that was formed in 2009, the Anglican Church in North America (ACNA). By 2022, ACNA had nearly one thousand churches with more than 120,000 members on its rolls.[4]

Our congregation was a mix of students who were burned out on their previous evangelical church experiences and a handful of ultra-wealthy conservative Episcopalians who sought an Anglican alternative to the liberal drift in their former congregations. We were there for the first service led by a highly regarded, well-educated new rector. There was a palpable sense that this congregation was committed to merging evangelical, charismatic, and small-c catholic tributaries in a traditionalist Anglican context. The experience of being a young mission church led by a bishop from Rwanda put all of us in a classroom, learning a new old way to be the church.

Of the four Reformation Protestant traditions (Lutheran, Calvinist, Mennonite, and Anglican) that emerged during the church's last rummage sale five hundred years ago, Anglicanism has the most colorful backstory. The origins of the Anglican Church were rooted in a break with the Catholic Church in 1534 when King Henry VIII declared himself the head of the Church of England in order to seek an annulment of his marriage to Catherine of Aragon. This political break created space for British religious leaders to begin reimagining the Reformation in their context under the headship of their own sovereign rather than the pope in Rome. They sought a "via media," a middle way, between Lutheranism

---

4. Ernie Didot, "Celebrating 15 Years of the ACNA," Anglican Church in North America, March 25, 2024, https://tinyurl.com/2th37c74.

Freedom in Leaving Most Everything Behind

and Catholicism. This commitment to a middle way is at the heart of the Anglican tradition.

Over time, Anglicanism birthed evangelical breakaway groups including the Methodists and the Plymouth Brethren. It has been the religious identity of eleven American presidents ranging from George Washington to George Herbert Walker Bush.[5] The Anglican tradition has fueled the writing of Charlotte Brontë, Jane Austen, Dorothy Sayers, Elizabeth Goudge, C. S. Lewis, and Jan Karon, and has been the theological home of contemporary evangelical voices including J. I. Packer, Stanley Hauerwas, Alister McGrath, N. T. Wright, John Stott, and Robert Webber.

Webber wrote about his journey, from a childhood with evangelical missionaries to a college career at fundamentalist bastion, Bob Jones University, to the Episcopal Church in his 1989 book, *Evangelicals on the Canterbury Trail: Why Evangelicals Are Attracted to the Liturgical Church*. He captured the longings of many evangelicals who'd made their way to Anglican congregations:

> For me, Anglicanism preserves in its worship and sacraments the sense of mystery that rationalistic Christianity of either the liberal or evangelical sort seems to deny. I found myself longing for an experience of worship that went beyond either emotionalism or intellectualism. I believe I've found that for myself in the Anglican tradition. I also felt a need for visible and tangible symbols that I could touch, feel, and experience with my senses. That need is met in the reality of Christ presented to me in the sacraments. These three needs—mystery, worship, and sacraments—are closely related.
>
> At times, I also felt like an ecclesiastical orphan looking for spiritual parents and a spiritual identity. I am now discov-

---

5. Aleksandra Sandstrom, "Biden Is Only the Second Catholic President, but Nearly All Have Been Christians," Pew Research Center, January 20, 2021, https://tinyurl.com/3cjzzwnj.

Chapter 10

ering my spiritual identity with all God's people throughout history, by embracing the church universal and a holistic perspective on spirituality. These three needs—historic identity, an ecclesiastical home, and a holistic spirituality—are also closely related.[6]

I'd wept a few times in church services over the years, because I'd heard a moving testimony or sensed a conviction of my own distance from God. But I'd never cried in a church service because the liturgy touched the kind of needs Webber described until our first visit to the tiny Anglican congregation. The word "liturgy" means "the work of the people." I leaned into the rhythms of liturgy; those rhythms called the congregation to worship, highlighted lectionary selections that were read aloud, invited me to confess my sins, called me to prayer, created space for a short sermon connected to the readings, and centered communion in our reason for gathering. Bits of Anglican liturgy seemed to echo the Jewish liturgy familiar to me from my childhood and time in Messianic congregations. The Book of Common Prayer, the foundation for Anglican liturgy, had been created in the early days of the English Reformation, and first refined by Archbishop Thomas Cranmer. Five centuries of occasional updating and refreshing of that original had not overwritten Cranmer's poetic, orthodox worship. Many evangelicals who found their way into older Christian traditions were renewed by reconnecting with a church history that predated Billy Graham.

I also appreciated the anchoring of the community to the Nicene Creed. Though much of evangelicalism was based on a "no creed but the Bible" orientation, Bill and I appreciated the way in which the ancient creeds distill the essentials of the faith. In fact, when we were living in Wisconsin, our family memorized

6. Robert E. Webber, *Evangelicals on the Canterbury Trail: Why Evangelicals Are Attracted to the Liturgical Church*, 2nd ed. (Harrisburg, PA: Morehouse, 1989, 2013), xix.

Freedom in Leaving Most Everything Behind

the even older Apostles' Creed as a way of helping us clarify what mattered most when we were searching for a new church.

The connection to history and tradition was rich and profound. Anglican rector Alex Wilgus noted:

> That period of the first five centuries contains the seeds of all of the familiar emphases of the many traditions we have today. The Reformed emphasis on the freedom and sovereignty of God, the Wesleyan yearning for holiness, the Catholic focus on the sacramental life, the Charismatic expectation that God remains supernaturally active in the Holy Spirit. It makes sense that an emphasis on the early church brings traditions together, since we are all descended from that common heritage. Like tributaries of a river that has hit rocks and is running apart, we all find our source in that same stream.[7]

For decades in evangelicalism, the only narrative to which I'd been exposed came from the stories of those who'd left their Catholic and mainline Protestant churches after they'd been born again. But the downsizing process has been changing that narrative. There may still be a flow into evangelicalism (albeit at a much slower rate than in the second half of the twentieth century), but there has also been a steady stream into mainline traditions from evangelicalism, and a disaffiliation from institutional religion that is changing the calculus in every Christian tradition. A 2024 Public Religion Research Institute study about church switching revealed:

> Approximately 3% of Americans now identify as white evangelical Protestants though they were brought up in a different or no faith tradition, drawing mainly from former mainline/

---

7. Alex Wilgus, "A New Generation of Anglicans," Anglican Compass, December 12, 2022, https://tinyurl.com/3shv3xdt.

Chapter 10

non-evangelical Protestants (40%) and Catholics (35%). Roughly one in five of today's white evangelical Protestants (18%) were previously unaffiliated. Around 4% were previously other Christians or belonged to other non-Christian traditions.

About 3% of Americans who were raised in a different tradition now identify as mainline/non-evangelical Protestants. Among this group, 37% were previously Catholic, 30% were evangelical Protestants, 3% belonged to other Christian religions, and 5% belonged to other non-Christian traditions. Nearly two in ten of those who switched to identify as white mainline/non-evangelical Protestants were previously unaffiliated (18%).

Nearly one in five Americans (18%) left a religious tradition to enter the ranks of the religiously unaffiliated, over one-third of whom were Catholics (35%) and mainline/non-evangelical Protestants (35%). The ranks of unaffiliated switchers are less likely to be drawn from former evangelical Protestants (16%), other non-Christian traditions (8%), or other Christian traditions.[8]

Here We Go Again

Our Anglican congregation was connected to a larger denominational structure, complete with layers of leadership hierarchy that stretched across the ocean to Rwanda, to Canterbury, and ultimately, all the way to Buckingham Palace. After the abuses we'd witnessed in almost every stream of nondenominational evangelicalism in which we'd splashed to this point, Bill and I dared to hope that structures external to a local congregation might provide oversight and serve to check the temptations that accompanied power.

8. "Religious Change in America," Public Religion Research Institute, March 27, 2024, https://tinyurl.com/yvxb9j9m.

Freedom in Leaving Most Everything Behind

Yet I was not naive. I had my own story of abuse. I well knew that abuse happened in large, sprawling denominations as well as in tiny independent nondenominational churches. I was familiar with the Spotlight investigative series done by the *Boston Globe* newspaper that had uncovered massive cover-ups of abusers in the Catholic Church. I'd followed the advocacy work that Survivors Network of those Abused by Priests (SNAP) had been doing since 1989. I knew that victims and survivors in Protestant and evangelical spaces were organizing and using their voices to bring to light what had been done to them in the shadows.

A historical spiritual pedigree, an elegant denominational structure, and a congregation full of wealthy and highly educated people can do little to curb the toxic impulses of a bad leader. We began to notice a pattern emerging in the congregation as a series of bright, attractive seminary students were first drawn into the rector's close social orbit and given plum roles of responsibility in the congregation, then after a while, without a word of explanation or a good-bye, each stopped attending even though still living in the area. We didn't know those who left well enough to ask any of them for their story, and other laypeople in the congregation didn't seem to know any more about their disappearance than we did. Eventually, Bill was invited to serve on the vestry, the group tasked with assisting the rector with church business decisions. Bill found himself unsettled by some of the ways the rector handled the congregation's finances. Were these things coincidences or warning signs?

Meanwhile, the housing market imploded in 2008, taking the US economy on an excruciating roller-coaster ride. By 2011, our home had lost two-thirds of its value, and we were so far underwater on our mortgage that it felt like we could touch the bottom of the sea. After prayer and consultation with a lawyer and a financial advisor, we elected to do a short sale on our house. When it was approved in 2012, we had less than ten days to move. God provided a rental property that was too far away to continue to attend the church. Leaving was a mixed bag for us. We loved the

Chapter 10

liturgy and the rhythms of the church year. And we carried some deep concerns about the rector. We knew something was off, but it would once again take a long, long time before the whole miserable, messed-up story came to the surface.

The abuse that had been happening in the shadows in just about every corner of evangelicalism for decades has been coming to light, thanks in large part to social media. Jesus said, "There is nothing concealed that will not be disclosed, or hidden that will not be made known. What you have said in the dark will be heard in the daylight, and what you have whispered in the ear in the inner rooms will be proclaimed from the roofs" (Luke 12:2–3). Victim advocates including lawyers Christa Brown, Rachael Denhollander, and Boz Tchividjian; Bible teacher Beth Moore; and whistleblowers Darlene Parsons and Julie Roys used their online platforms to bring to light abuse that had long festered in the darkness within denominations, megachurches, and other ministries.

These revelations were already unfolding at a steady clip when the #MeToo hashtag swept across pop culture in 2017 after actress Alyssa Milano invited others who'd experienced sexual assault or harassment in their workplace to stand up and be counted. More than 12 million people did so in the first twenty-four hours.[9] It didn't take long before #MeToo became #ChurchToo, and more victims of abusive Christian leaders found one another online and formed communities of support. Others were empowered to begin speaking publicly about their experiences and begin advocating for justice.

Among them were some of the individuals who'd left our former congregation. Eventually, a third-party firm hired to investigate the rector issued a damning report that detailed his inappropriate relationships, his manipulation of those in his inner circle, his alcohol abuse, his financial irregularities, and more. He resigned and was defrocked in 2022.

---

9. Holly Corbett, "#MeToo Five Years Later: How the Movement Started and What Needs to Change," *Forbes*, October 27, 2022, https://tinyurl.com/4df289t7.

Freedom in Leaving Most Everything Behind

This unfolded as other cases within ACNA were coming to light, including that of a Chicago-area bishop who was accused of spiritual abuse and mishandling the case of Mark Rivera, a serial sex offender the bishop has personally placed in ministry. As of this writing, the case against the bishop is still being litigated by Anglican leaders.[10] Rivera is currently serving a twenty-one-year prison sentence after he was found guilty of multiple counts of child sexual abuse.[11]

It has been gut-wrenching to realize that clergy sexual abuse and abuse of power have marked almost every place in which I've sojourned in the American evangelical community. I have cried, "This is not what I signed up for, Lord!"

Frankly, this is not what any of us signed up for.

Whether we were victims of this evil or simply witnessed its effect from afar, each one of us has been affected. The church is not who she should be or must be. She needs to be born again, and the only way to get there is via downsizing.

Downsizing: Freedom in Leaving Most Everything Behind

In the wake of the short sale of our home in 2012, Bill and I ended up having four addresses in seven years. It was an ongoing seminar in the process of downsizing. As difficult as it was, the process also taught me that there was freedom ahead. Fewer possessions made room for what God had next for us. We didn't need a big house to serve as a museum for our past, nor as a symbol of aspiration for a future that was no longer wise or financially possible. Downsizing gave us clarity about what we really needed for our future. It turns out, it wasn't much.

10. Kathryn Post, "Anglican Bishop Removed as Clergy Call for Transparency in Investigation," *Christianity Today*, May 22, 2024, https://tinyurl.com/4fe4npk9.

11. Kathryn Post, "Mark Rivera Pleads Guilty to Felony Sexual Assault, Sentenced to 6 More Years," *Ministry Watch*, April 13, 2023, https://tinyurl.com/5n9bzjzy.

Chapter 10

There was much bright expectation among many evangelicals (including us) about the rise of the Anglican church. Finally, a rich, intellectually challenging way in which to remain evangelical while being anchored to tradition and bathed in the beauty of "smells and bells" high-church worship! Many of us who found our way to congregations like the one we attended experienced the church as our classroom. We may have imagined we were enrolled in the coursework that would teach us how to be evangelical the Anglican way. But the real lessons came as many discovered that no matter what form the church took, there was no refuge from a wolf acting as a leader, whether the wolf dressed in formal clerical vestments or skinny jeans and sneakers. Our sanctuary is in God alone.

What might remain from this evangelical era in the downsized church of the future? We should not be surprised to discover that it might not be where we've invested so much of our energies.

But I am convinced that what survives after the downsizing process does its work in the church will be pure gold and will endure to the end of days.

Reflect

1.   Evangelicalism is not known for its connection to tradition or the flow of church history. What has the movement forfeited by this lack of connection? What has it gained?

2.   If you've been in a congregation that has been marked by clergy sexual abuse and cover-up, what has the effect been on your faith? (Also, please note that the appendix at the end of this book offers some resources if you are looking for help and a way forward from your experience.)

3.   What do you think will remain in the church from the evangelicalism that has emerged since the Jesus Movement in the late 1960s?

Conclusion: Bride

A lifetime ago, I sat around a campfire at a beach on a warm summer night with eight or ten other teen friends. One of the guys just baptized a girl in the August-warmed water of the lake. Another guy was strumming his guitar, and the rest of us were singing "Pass It On." We ended our evening with an impromptu communion service, passing around some damp salted crackers and taking swigs of warm juice from a communal thermos.

More recently, I found myself sitting in an old wooden pew on a Sunday morning, listening as the paid professional choir sang a stirring arrangement of a nineteenth-century hymn while being accompanied by a thundering pipe organ. Sunlight illuminated the stained-glass windows rimming the sanctuary. There was a baptism during the service. An ordained member of the clergy sprinkled the baby with holy water from a font, as the parents and godparents committed to raising the child in the faith. That same clergyperson officiated over the Eucharist later in the service, offering each congregant an unleavened wafer and sip of wine from an elegant golden vessel, with the words, "The body of Christ, broken for you; the blood of Christ, shed for you."

Conclusion

I have found the church in those places, as well as in the start-up congregation in the rented school gym, among the throng sitting in a state-of-the-art amphitheater the size of an airplane hangar, and with a graying group worshiping in a storefront church.

My early impression of what the church was supposed to be—a container that held individual born-again believers—was drawn from the way we used the word "church" in the English language. The word "church" is most frequently used to name our physical gathering spaces and denominational affiliations. Those things are nothing more than containers. They aren't the church the way the Bible speaks about it.

The Greek word used in the New Testament for church is *ekklēsia*, which means "called-out assembly." It was used in Greek culture to describe political meetings, but in the Bible, it is applied specifically to gatherings of those called to follow Jesus. It is translated "church," but it describes the community of believers and is never used to define the form it should take. And unlike the specific descriptions in the Old Testament of the tabernacle or temple, there are no detailed instructions about what the physical worship space or the liturgy of the *ekklēsia* is supposed to look like. Paul's paradigm-shifting words to his friends in Corinth underscore this reality: "Don't you know that you yourselves are God's temple and that God's Spirit dwells in your midst? If anyone destroys God's temple, God will destroy that person; for God's temple is sacred, and you together are that temple" (1 Cor. 3:16–17). We find the New Testament *ekklēsia* gathering in all sorts of settings, including in homes (Acts 2:46; Rom. 16:5; 1 Cor. 16:19; Col. 4:15), in the courts of the temple in Jerusalem (Acts 2:47), along the bank of a river (Acts 16:13), and inside a prison cell (Acts 16:25–26).

Scripture reminds us in 1 Corinthians 12 that the church is far greater than the sum of its separate parts and was never meant to be defined by the shape of the container in which she gathers. At the end of days, the whole *ekklēsia* steps into her penultimate identity—that of the bride of Christ. Using both parable and di-

Bride

dactic teaching, Jesus referred to himself as a bridegroom during his earthly ministry (Matt. 9:15; 25:1–13; Mark 2:19–20; Luke 5:34–35; John 3:29). The final scenes in the book of Revelation are of a wedding celebration: the bride, the church pure and whole. She is a beautiful composite of believers from every tongue, tribe, and nation, throughout all of time, given as one to the Son.

What forms each one of us and all of us together to become a part of that beautiful, living bride?

In a word: Downsizing.

Downsizing is the essence of discipleship: in response to Jesus's "Follow me," each of his followers had to leave something of their old lives behind. What got left behind varied by individual and included things core to a person's identity as vocation, family, lifestyle, ideas, or possessions. Additionally, God uses the tests and trials of our lives in this turbulent world to liberate us from our self-reliance and nurture our trust in him, even when we are stepping into an unknown future. Maybe especially when we are journeying into the unknown. Downsizing frees us to follow him.

I respect the doctrinal distinctions that have shaped different Protestant streams and traditions. I understand on an intellectual level why some groups would reject the impromptu baptism service a bunch of Jesus freak teenagers had at a lake, and why others would question whether only an ordained clergyperson could preside over communion. There's history surrounding these convictions, and plenty of complicated stories about how God's people have either engaged in the hard work of hammering out their theological differences or chosen to divide from one another when there was no clear compromise between two factions.

But the church is bigger than our doctrinal convictions. The church is wider than our division. The church is more resilient than our theological errors. The church is more enduring than our toxic practices.

The bride will be refined in this current round of downsizing just as she has been in each of the previous ones over the last two

Conclusion

thousand years. The story of Christian history as told through the actions of popes and pastors and monarchs and generals may be described in history books, but the real treasure of the church is found in the spiritual children of those whose names aren't well known except to God: two mothers interceding for their prodigal children, a doctor who travels to a conflict zone to provide care in the name of Jesus, a musician singing hymns in an Alzheimer's unit of a nursing home, a Christian foster mom caring for a drug addict's baby, or an ex-con leading a weekly Bible study in a prison. The Christian history that matters is found in the stories of people who have seen their lives transformed by the love of God.

But there is no denying that the One who separates the wheat from the tares is at work in this current moment of sifting and downsizing in evangelicalism in America and the West. Downsizing is an expression of his love, too.

Will we cooperate with him? Will we receive God's correction and redirection?

I've been a witness to many different streams of evangelicalism that might not appear at first to have much in common. But on closer examination, more than a few have been characterized by theology and practice formed around the craving for power and control. That craving is not limited to leaders. There is a symbiotic relationship between authoritarian leaders and the followers who are drawn to the many different types of authoritarian religious systems within evangelicalism. I recognize that my own story is that of a person longing for belonging. As a result, my story has chapters where I've been a willing participant in what I now recognize as toxic systems, and has other chapters where I've been a wounded observer trying to make sense of what I've experienced while fighting to hang on to my faith in God.

I am not alone. I've talked to many people throughout the last two decades who have their own confusing, painful horror stories from their time in evangelical churches. Of one thing I'm certain: what will survive from evangelicalism will be emptied of our de-

Bride

pendence on abusive authority, institutional loyalty, and noxious, shallow theological innovation. Are we ready to imagine a future that might not contain a whole lot of what has dominated this movement during the last half century?

Scripture uses powerful language to describe the church that is linked to the good desires God himself has hard-wired into the spiritual DNA of his people. Those desires existed before evangelicalism first sprouted, and they will continue to shape the future of the church universal, even if evangelicalism is pruned all the way down to its root:

- The parachurch—the desire for meaningful, committed community
- The priesthood of all believers—the desire to learn how to live in sacrificial service to God and others
- Messianic Judaism—the desire to embrace Scripture's whole story of relationship with God and mission to the world
- Shepherding teaching—the desire for protection and security
- Third-wave charismatic renewal—the desire for wholeness
- The homeschool movement—the desire to pass on a living faith among the next generation
- The church growth movement—the desire for order and purpose
- The New Apostolic Reformation—the desire for spiritual power and to be a part of something bigger than the individual
- Preevangelical forms of church—the desire for the joy of worship and delight of intellectual as well as spiritual engagement

Much of this book reads like a lament, and indeed it is. So much has gone so wrong in evangelicalism. There isn't a lot of lasting value in the movements and institutions in which we've invested so much of our energy. As a result, there is much we need to grieve.

But ultimately, lament is an expression of desire for a different future. Our cries of anguish are what give us ears to hear what

Conclusion

God is saying to us at this moment in time—and what he has been saying throughout history.

In the end, the refined bride, downsized to purity and living beyond time, calls with one voice in unison with the Spirit to us whom he calls his treasure: "The Spirit and the bride say, 'Come!' And let the one who hears say, 'Come!' Let the one who is thirsty come; and let the one who wishes take the free gift of the water of life" (Rev. 22:17).

Appendix:
Spiritual Trauma Resources

A study done by the Global Center for Religious Research suggests that about a third of all adults in the United States have likely experienced religious trauma at some point in their lives, and about 10–15 percent are currently experiencing an active case of religious trauma. It defines religious trauma as the result of "an event, series of events, relationships, or circumstances within or connected to religious beliefs, practices, or structures that is experienced by an individual as overwhelming or disruptive and has lasting adverse effects on a person's physical, mental, social, emotional, or spiritual well-being." This trauma may manifest itself in a wide variety of ways including (but not limited to) a deep sense of shame about not living up to expectations; fear of rejection by God or a faith community; anxiety about the rapture, hell, demonic influence; hypervigilance; difficulty experiencing pleasure; shame about one's body or sexuality.[1]

---

1. "Results from the World's First, Most Exhaustive Sociological Study on Religious Trauma," GCRR, accessed October 7, 2024, https://tinyurl.com/ycchexrm.

Appendix

If you've experienced clergy sexual abuse or spiritual abuse, or are carrying religious trauma after being in a high-control church environment, please know that you are not alone. This list of resources is not comprehensive. It is meant to offer you a starting place as you process your own experience or seek to lend support to others.

Books

- *The Body Keeps the Score: Brain, Mind, and Body in the Healing of Trauma*, by Bessel van der Kolk (Penguin, 2014).
- *Church Called Tov: Forming a Goodness Culture That Resists Abuses of Power and Promotes Healing*, by Scot McKnight and Laura Barringer (Tyndale, 2020).
- *Emotionally Healthy Discipleship: Moving from Shallow Christianity to Deep Transformation*, by Peter Scazzero (Zondervan, 2021).
- *The Lord Is My Courage: Stepping through the Shadows of Fear toward the Voice of Love*, by K. J. Ramsey (Zondervan, 2022).
- *Redeeming Power: Understanding Abuse and Authority in the Church*, by Diane Langberg (Brazos, 2020).
- *When Narcissism Comes to Church: Healing Your Community from Emotional and Spiritual Abuse*, by Chuck DeGroat (InterVarsity Press, 2020).

Organizations

Each of these organizations can be found on the Web.

- Christian Trauma Healing Network—provides training and opportunities for collaboration among counseling professionals, pastors, and laypeople.
- National Alliance for Mental Illness—offers mental health resources, including courses, support groups, and much more.

Spiritual Trauma Resources

- Net Grace—this advocacy group trains churches to recognize and respond to abuse and provides assistance to victims.

- Trauma Informed Churches—offers online training to church leaders to equip them and their congregations to more sensitively care for those who've experienced trauma, including sexual abuse and rape, imprisoned parents, domestic abuse, bullying, and more.

In addition, many of these organizations may be able to provide a referral to a counselor who has experience in issues relating to religious trauma and abuse.

Acknowledgments

Once upon a time, I remember hearing some church leaders speak disparagingly of "church hoppers" who couldn't commit long-term to a congregational home. While there may be some who move from church to church in a consumerist search for a congregation that fits their doctrinal preferences, musical tastes, or programming desires, I have found that most who have wandered from church to church aren't looking for the perfect congregation—they're longing for one that is faithful. The courageous pilgrim souls I've encountered on every step of my journey through evangelicalism have showed me that I'm not the only one who has had the kinds of experiences I have described in this book. There are too many to name. I couldn't have written this book without any one of them.

As I remember each of the churches that have formed me, both the ones I named throughout these pages and the many others I've visited through the years, I recognize that when each one of these congregations and movements began, there was a desire among each of the founders to respond in some new way to what they sensed the Spirit was doing that drew spiritually hungry people

165

Acknowledgments

like me into their ranks. Some organizations have done lasting good as they've served God, their members and attenders, and their communities. I am profoundly thankful for the quiet witness of those who are committed to do justice, love mercy, and walk humbly with God. These siblings in faith have kept me from spiraling into despair as I've continued to witness so much moral failure among so many evangelical leaders in addition to a stunning amount of warped teaching and practice in many different streams of the church.

I honor the people who've shepherded me through critical passages in my life, though none has ever had the title "pastor": Pam Hill, Karen Ewen, Ginnie Lange, Meg Kausalik, Cricket Giles, Diane Siri, Carol Marshall, Janet Davis, Melinda Schmidt, and Anita Murphy.

I am grateful for the communities of wordsmiths and communicators with whom I've connected online (and sometimes in real life), including friendship that began way back in the days when I was a regular contributor to *Christianity Today*'s late, lamented *Her.meneutics* blog. INK writers continue to be an encouragement to me, particularly Susy Flory, who was the first person with whom I shared the idea for *Downsizing*. Her affirmation was enough to bring me to the blank screen and blinking cursor to begin writing. The women of the Pelican Project have prayed for me and supported me throughout the process. And I am grateful for the generosity of Dave Schmidt, who shared his experience and expertise in the early stages of drafting this book.

My agent, Steve Laube, has been a champion of my efforts for several years, and I am deeply grateful to him. I'm also grateful to the crew at Eerdmans, including Andrew Knapp, Jenny Hoffman, and Tom Raabe. Their professionalism is an expression of their care.

When Bill and I married forty-five years ago, neither of us could have ever imagined that I'd become a writer. And I'm sure I wouldn't have stepped into that vocation without his unselfish

Acknowledgments

encouragement and faithful support every step of the way. We have lived most of the story of *Downsizing* together, and I could not imagine anyone else who would persevere in faith through so many chaotic church experiences. While I believe that God can redeem anything, I grieve for what those experiences taught our beloved children about God and his people. They deserved better. We all did.

Revelation 21:4 echoes the prophetic promise found in Isaiah 25:8: "'He will wipe every tear from their eyes. There will be no more death' or mourning or crying or pain, for the old order of things has passed away." Lord Jesus, I am holding on to this hope.

Bibliography

Advanced Training Institute International. Application form. Accessed September 27, 2024. https://tinyurl.com/2xe5fvx7.

Akers, Shawn. "Lou Engle Sees Another Jesus Movement Rising." *Charisma*, March 9, 2016. https://tinyurl.com/3decye8n.

Arnott, John, and Carol Arnott. "The Toronto Blessing: What Is It?" *John and Carol* (blog), December 31, 1999. https://tinyurl.com/5aw96m8d.

Baer, Brooks. "Religious Trauma: Signs, Symptoms, Causes, and Treatment." Therapist.com, May 16, 2024. https://tinyurl.com/5tkv5h3r.

Banks, Adelle M. "The Key Evangelical Players on Trump's Advisory Board." *National Catholic Reporter*, September 5, 2017. https://tinyurl.com/4s9chufw.

Bass, Diana Butler. "I Don't Understand." Dianabutlerbass.substack.com, January 25, 2024. https://tinyurl.com/55p5s6cx.

Bebbington, David. "What Is Revivalism?" *Christianity Today*. Accessed September 27, 2024. https://tinyurl.com/mr2bdu34.

Bennett, Dennis. "God's Strength for This Generation." HealMyLife.com. Accessed September 27, 2024. https://tinyurl.com/47bnmhdx.

Bibliography

Beverley, James A. "Leading Church Leaves Association." *Christianity Today*, October 7, 1996. https://tinyurl.com/3x4jca8e.

Bonhoeffer, Dietrich. *Letters and Papers from Prison*. New York: Simon & Schuster, 2011.

"A Brief History of Homeschooling." Coalition for Responsible Homeschooling. Accessed September 27, 2024. https://tinyurl.com/yfbv4dun.

Burge, Ryan P. "Can You Be an Evangelical and Never Go to Church?" *Religion in Public*, May 18, 2020. https://tinyurl.com/55hj5b4a.

Burke, Katie, and Linda Moss. "Why Retailers Are Abandoning Traditional Malls." *CoStar*, May 22, 2023. https://tinyurl.com/mwcdrr9u.

Corbett, Holly. "#MeToo Five Years Later: How the Movement Started and What Needs to Change." *Forbes*, October 27, 2022. https://tinyurl.com/4df289t7.

Daniels, David D. "Why Pentecostalism's Multiethnic Beginning Floundered." *Christianity Today*. Accessed September 27, 2024. https://tinyurl.com/2a2cj3xw.

"The Danvers Statement." Council on Biblical Manhood and Womanhood. Accessed September 27, 2024. https://tinyurl.com/2d56rys9.

Davis, Jim, Michael Graham, and Ryan Burge. *The Great Dechurching: Who's Leaving, Why Are They Going, and What Will It Take to Bring Them Back?* Grand Rapids: Zondervan, 2023.

DeHaan, Peter. "What Happened to the Emergent Church?" Peterdehaan.com, April 13, 2022. https://tinyurl.com/3ndhs4tn.

Didot, Ernie. "Celebrating 15 Years of the ACNA." Anglican Church in North America, March 25, 2024. https://tinyurl.com/2th37c74.

"Disruption: Past and Future." Fuller Studio. Accessed September 27, 2024. https://tinyurl.com/awset8z4.

Dubov, Nissan Dovid. "The Chosen People: Chosen for What?" Chabad.org. Accessed September 27, 2024. https://tinyurl.com/3d7b9m58.

Duin, Julia. "Pentecostalism from Soup to Nuts: A (Near) Complete

Bibliography

History of This Movement in America." Get Religion, February 2, 2023. https://tinyurl.com/3f738eb9.

Engelkemier, Joe. "A Church That Draws Thousands." *Ministry*, May 1991. https://tinyurl.com/4xcd93pw.

Gray, Kyle. "The Decline of White Evangelical Protestants." Survey Center on American Life, October 7, 2022. https://tinyurl.com/355m2tmy.

Gross, Jessica. "The Largest and Fastest Religious Shift in America Is Well Underway." *New York Times*, June 21, 2023. https://tinyurl.com/277hsa88.

[Gross, Terry]. "A Leading Figure in the New Apostolic Reformation." NPR, October 3, 2011. https://tinyurl.com/5n6zx48p.

Harris, Brian. "Beyond Bebbington: The Quest for Evangelical Identity in a Postmodern Era." Theology on the Web. Accessed September 27, 2024. https://tinyurl.com/3rutrxah.

Harris, Joshua. *I Kissed Dating Goodbye*. Sisters, OR: Multnomah, 1997.

Hinson, Keith. "Evangelism: To the Jew First?" *Christianity Today*, November 15, 1999. https://tinyurl.com/24wpjbwr.

"Homeschooling in the United States: 1999." National Center for Education Statistics. Accessed September 27, 2024. https://tinyurl.com/2whs2685.

"How Do You Define a Denomination?" Center for the Study of Global Christianity at Gordon-Conwell Theological Seminary. Accessed September 27, 2024. https://tinyurl.com/yupzes2.

Hybels, Bill, and Lynne Hybels. *Rediscovering Church: The Story and Vision of Willow Creek Church*. Grand Rapids: Zondervan, 1995.

Keillor, Garrison. *Lake Wobegon Days*. New York: Viking, 1985.

Kidd, Thomas. *Who Is an Evangelical? The History of a Movement in Crisis*. New Haven: Yale University Press, 2019.

Lazarus, David. "Messianic Jews in the World Today." *Israel Today*, April 20, 2021. https://tinyurl.com/23nc9t65.

Lecaque, Thomas. "The Twisted, Trumpist Religion of Jan. 6th." *Bulwark*, January 6, 2022. https://tinyurl.com/2p8mwvyc.

Luther, Martin. "First Sunday after Epiphany." In *Complete Sermons of Martin Luther*, vol. 4. Grand Rapids: Baker Books, 2007.

Bibliography

Marshall, Peter J., and David Manuel Jr. *The Light and the Glory*. Grand Rapids: Revell, 1977, 2009.

McGavran, Donald. *Bridges of God: A Study in the Strategy of Missions*. New York: Friendship, 1955.

McKnight, Scot. "Revivalism: What Is It?" *Scot's Newsletter*, March 3, 2022. https://tinyurl.com/3hfk2d6m.

Meador, Jake. "American Evangelicalism as a Controversy Generator Machine." *Mere Orthodoxy*, February 6, 2024. https://tinyurl.com/bp9x4epw.

"Megachurch Definition." Hartford Institute for Religion Research. Accessed September 27, 2024. https://tinyurl.com/44bwfkbm.

Moore, Art. "Spiritual Mapping Gains Credibility among Leaders." *Christianity Today*, January 12, 1998. https://tinyurl.com/3n7jzdxe.

Morley, Patrick. "A Brief History of Spiritual Revival and Awakening in America." *Church Leaders*, October 12, 2022. https://tinyurl.com/2z72addr.

"The New Face of Global Christianity: The Emergence of 'Progressive Pentecostalism.'" Pew Research Center, April 12, 2006. https://tinyurl.com/6ryh842t.

Olson, Roger E. "What Distinguishes 'Evangelical' from 'Fundamentalist'?" *Patheos*, December 2, 2017. https://tinyurl.com/5xmxe9zu.

"People of Jewish Background and Jewish Affinity." Pew Research Center, May 11, 2021. https://tinyurl.com/mryzmd9h.

Plowman, Edward E. "Bill Gothard's Institute." *Christianity Today*, May 25, 1973. https://tinyurl.com/yxyurrmr.

Post, Kathryn. "Anglican Bishop Removed as Clergy Call for Transparency in Investigation." *Christianity Today*, May 22, 2024. https://tinyurl.com/4fe4npk9.

———. "Mark Rivera Pleads Guilty to Felony Sexual Assault, Sentenced to 6 More Years." *Ministry Watch*, April 13, 2023. https://tinyurl.com/5n9bzjzy.

"Quotes from John Wimber." Vineyard USA. Accessed September 27, 2024. https://tinyurl.com/ytj6rt8u.

Bibliography

"Religious Change in America." Public Religion Research Institute, March 27, 2024. https://tinyurl.com/yvxb9j9m.

Romano, Aja, Alissa Wilkinson, and Emily St. James. "Revisiting the Christian Fantasy Novels That Shaped Decades of Conservative Hysteria." *Vox*, April 28, 2022. https://tinyurl.com/3txyvn2b.

Rozet, Dmitry. "The Word of Faith Movement and Positive Confession." SATS, October 23, 2020. https://tinyurl.com/yc5fpdh3.

Sandstrom, Aleksandra. "Biden Is Only the Second Catholic President, but Nearly All Have Been Christians." Pew Research Center, January 20, 2021. https://tinyurl.com/3cjzzwnj.

"The Seven Mountains of Societal Influence." Generals International. Accessed September 27, 2024. https://tinyurl.com/3dxd96x6.

Shaffer, Kent. "Why Megachurches Keep Growing." Preach It Teach It. Accessed September 27, 2024. https://tinyurl.com/599n7dn9.

"660 Million Evangelicals in the World?" Evangelical Focus: Europe, February 18, 2020. https://tinyurl.com/rdrat6xt.

Smietana, Bob. "The 'Prophets' and 'Apostles' Leading the Quiet Revolution in American Religion." *Christianity Today*, August 3, 2017. https://tinyurl.com/yckak69f.

Stafford, Tim, and Jim Beverley. "God's Wonder Worker." *Christianity Today*, July 14, 1997. https://tinyurl.com/yc57fdd3.

Stetzer, Ed. *The Evolution of Church Growth, Church Health, and the Missional Church: An Overview of the Church Growth Movement from, and Back to, Its Missional Roots. Christianity Today* online archive. Accessed May 23, 2024.

Synan, Vinson. "Pentecostalism: William Seymour." Christian History Institute. Accessed September 27, 2024. https://tinyurl.com/22rb9ucc.

Tickle, Phyllis. *Emergence Christianity: What It Is, Where It's Going, and Why It Matters*. Grand Rapids: Baker Books, 2012.

"Top 50 Books That Have Shaped Evangelicals." *Christianity Today*, October 2006. https://tinyurl.com/y82y9jk7.

Wagner, C. Peter. *Apostles Today: Biblical Government for Biblical Power*. Bloomington, MN: Chosen Books, 2006.

Bibliography

"We Are Designed to Be Spiritual Creatures." Beliefnet. Accessed September 27, 2024. https://tinyurl.com/y4k2kz4n.

Weaver, John. *The New Apostolic Reformation: History of a Modern Charismatic Movement.* Jefferson, NC: McFarland & Co., 2016.

Webber, Robert E. *Evangelicals on the Canterbury Trail: Why Evangelicals Are Attracted to the Liturgical Church.* 2nd ed. Harrisburg, PA. Morehouse, 1989, 2013.

"What Is an Evangelical?" National Association of Evangelicals. Accessed September 27, 2024. https://tinyurl.com/yk97rz2t.

"What Is the Vineyard? Our History." Vineyard USA. Accessed September 27, 2024. https://tinyurl.com/mu36bey5.

"What *Reveal* Reveals." Editorial. *Christianity Today*, March 2008. https://tinyurl.com/yc7p5sws.

"Who Is a Jew: Matrilineal Descent." My Jewish Learning. Accessed September 27, 2024. https://tinyurl.com/kamtd5wv.

Wilgus, Alex. "A New Generation of Anglicans." Anglican Compass, December 12, 2022. https://tinyurl.com/3shv3xdt.

Williams, Chad. "A 'Hospital for Sinners'? (Re-thinking 'Equipping' in the Church)." Develop to Deploy, October 18, 2021. https://tinyurl.com/ywj75ttk.

Womack, Nathan. "Charismatic Renewal Movement in Christianity: Second Wave Pentecostalism." University of British Columbia, August 10, 2020. https://tinyurl.com/3acmp4p6.

Zavada, Jack. "Word of Faith Movement History." Learn Religions, updated December 10, 2018. https://tinyurl.com/3pbvf2ds.

Zylstra, Sarah Eekhoff. "1 in 3 American Evangelicals Is a Person of Color." *Christianity Today*, September 6, 2017. https://tinyurl.com/2bjwbb3v.

About the Author

Michelle Van Loon, in high school in 1976, giving a speech about the history of Passover and how it connects to Jesus

Michelle Van Loon has been writing and speaking about Jesus for more than fifty years. To learn more about her work, visit www.michellevanloon.com or subscribe to her free monthly newsletter, Transforming Words, at michellevanloon.substack.com.